The Road Trip –

The Bloke's Bible

For Jonathan, for putting up with thirty years of me –
from Ellery Queen to Alan Partridge. David and
Jonathan, friends and brothers.
And for my Ma and Da – for always believing, always
praying, always encouraging me.
Thank you.

The Road Trip –

The Bloke's Bible

Dave Hopwood

Authentic

LONDON • COLORADO SPRINGS • HYDERABAD

Copyright © 2007 Dave Hopwood

13 12 11 10 09 08 07   8 7 6 5 4 3 2 1

First published 2007 by Authentic Media
9 Holdom Avenue, Bletchley, Milton Keynes, MK1 1QR, UK
1820 Jet Stream Drive, Colorado Springs, CO 80921, USA
OM Authentic Media, Medchal Road, Jeedimetla Village,
Secunderabad 500 055, A.P., India
www.authenticmedia.co.uk

Authentic Media is a division of IBS-STL U.K., limited by guarantee, with
its Registered Office at Kingstown Broadway, Carlisle, Cumbria CA3 0HA.
Registered in England & Wales No. 1216232. Registered charity 270162

British Library Cataloguing in Publication Data
A catalogue record for this book is available from the British Library

ISBN-13: 978-1-85078-753-2
ISBN-10: 1-85078-753-0

Cover Design by David Smart
Print Management by Adare Carwin
Printed in Great Britain by J.H. Haynes & Co., Sparkford

Contents

Foreword

'What is manly about being a Christian?' What is 'manly' at all these days? Western culture struggles to identify what it means to be a man. Women have made a lot of progress in rediscovering what it is to be a woman. Because of this men can no longer simply determine manliness in terms of running companies, ruling countries, showing sporting prowess or engaging in extreme acts of derring-do, like sailing solo round the world. Women do all these things now, sometimes better. No longer are there many exclusive male experiences.

Our culture says 'real men' are good-looking, dangerous, muscular sportsmen – with a caring, sensitive side. 'Real men' pull on designer shirts over their well-toned bodies, before taking their children to school and going on to that well-paid job in a nice car. They are perfect fathers, skilled lovers and materially successful. If that's a real man, I don't know many . . . any?

The reality for most of us is that we don't like to remove the shirt as it reveals the less than perfect body. We struggle to juggle the expectations of family, job and social life and we dare not examine ourselves too closely because we all know the imperfections that lurk beneath. What's manly about that?

The Bible, on the other hand, doesn't hide from the imperfections of 'real men', nor does it spin the facts to present the heroes of our faith as perfect human beings. The Bible presents men as real, imperfect, flawed, gruesome yet glorious. And God loves them. God forgives them. God sends them out there as they are and uses them there and then. Cain, Abram, Jacob, Jeremiah, Peter were all men, living life in all its fullness with all their imperfections, and yet God still used their faith, their gifts and – often – their faults. These men were on adventures for God – sometimes dangerous, nearly always difficult and full of the common emotions of lust, anger, pain and love. They laughed, cried, succeeded and failed. The Bible shows us that being a man is not rocket-science but it can be hard, risky, dangerous, fantastic, and a bit of a laugh.

I've known Dave for several years and I have always found him to have a tremendous gift for reconnecting us with the reality of the characters we read about in the Bible, bringing them into the *Big Brother* culture and exposing them for who they are: real men with real issues, just like us.

In this, his second book about the blokes of the Bible, Dave's character leaves the warm comfort of home and drives on an adventure, seeking release from the responsibilities of life. But the Road Trip away from family, work and home brings him up sharp against his own imperfections and failings, gives him space to reflect and to read his battered old Bible. In it, he finds not some 'holy book', but a collection of stories about real men working out their relationships with others and with God, just like him.

Dave's book will make you laugh, it will make you admit 'that's me', it will challenge you, it will make you think about life, God and belief. Above all, it will help you to feel real and really affirmed before God as a man. It will encourage you to see yourself as the kind of man who is a 'godly hero'.

If you like adventure, a good story and seek a 'real' godly manliness, this book will help. Thanks, Dave.

Enjoy!

Mat Ineson

Introduction

Ever wanted to get away from it all? Ever dreamt of just leaping in your car with a rucksack and driving off into the sunset? Well, this is it. This is the tale of a guy who gets to do just that. Escape all his fears, worries, responsibilities and work – if only for a few days. He takes with him his little black Bible and every so often throws it open to see what spills out. He stops whenever he feels like it and he does whatever he wants. For once the world is his oyster and he finds much of what he encounters reflected in his battered good book.

Like the previous Bloke's Bible, you'll see I have played fast and loose with the biblical text – we come to the Bible with so many strait-laced preconceptions. I wanted to do my best to paint a fuller, more contemporary picture of what might have been going on. And once again the stories are random and I've picked passages which lately have appealed to me. This is a guy who can't be bothered to be organised about Bible reading notes, he just wants a bit of the word whenever he wants it and in the order that he happens to find it.

I hope this book helps bring some of these stories alive for you, I hope it takes you on an adventure for a few days and most of all I hope it helps you see again the God who gave us laughter, friendship and purpose.

Dave Hopwood

1. Abram Goes AWOL

Genesis 12

When do you eat the last bit of bread in your possession? When you're fat and healthy, while your body's still able to make good use of it? Or d'you wait until the skin is hanging off your brittle bones and the muscles have melted away like wax? He's seen this day coming for a while, of course. No matter how much you pack for a long journey, sooner or later the rucksack'll be bare. His wife's hungry too, of course, so there'll be barely enough to go round. The servants haven't eaten in days. The concubines are losing their sheen by the hour.

Abram sits on a rock and wonders. Was it really such a good decision back there? Standing beneath that widescreen vista of a million stars, hearing that voice boom across the night like the roar of a celestial lion, it all went to his head. It was so thrilling then, made his spine shudder and his hair stand on end. The voice of God booming at him from the great Unknown. Those rich mellow tones of hope megaphoning their way across the universe right at him. Who wouldn't have been impressed, who wouldn't have expected the world to open up like a massive yielding oyster?

A camel grunts and spits behind him, he hears the glob of saliva land on the rock inches from his backside.

Abram turns and cusses at it. In the hot sunlight there are no stars in the sky: in the unwieldy daylight there is no promise of a future or a hope. What's he to do? Turn back and go home to a retirement of grumbling and sour memories? Or press on and see what's down in Egypt?

God never told him there'd be a famine. There was no mention of rumbling stomachs and carpet-pile tongues when all this began. Where are you now, God? Where are the gleaming promises? He scans the bright sky but there's nothing up there. Just the burning sun and an increasing number of ragged vultures.

Sarai slips down beside him and sighs. She's tired and hungry too but she's still so beautiful. He'll love her forever, he'll do anything to protect her from harm. It breaks his heart to see her suffering like this. And all because of him.

'We could be in Egypt in a couple of days,' she whispers, her almond eyes pleading for his agreement. 'It won't be giving up, Egypt won't be like turning back and going home.'

She smells perfect, she always smells that way. Even here in the desert heat when everyone else stinks like a camel's backside.

'They say he's a predator,' Abram mutters, flicking at the bits of dried blood that border the broken nail on his right thumb. 'They say he'll do anything to get his well-oiled paws on visiting women.'

She nods and there's a shudder about her body as she does it.

'God'll get us through it,' she says.

'Oh sure. Easy to say that when we're starving and looking over the fence at Egyptian corn. What will you say when you're pinned under the king's torso and I'm buried in his back yard?'

'Let's face that mountain when we have to . . .'

Abram laughs a cynical laugh but he still stands and turns his face towards Egypt.

Before they know it they're standing in front of Pharaoh and his dancing girls; the man's a giant lump of seeping lard – all mouth and no trousers.

He cuts an ugly figure, with a stomach like the side of a pyramid. He barely looks at Abram: he only has eyes for Sarai.

Abram feels the anger and fear collide in his empty stomach.

His eyes burn like lasers into the king's neck but Pharaoh couldn't care less. He's got a vacancy in his harem and Sarai has the perfect credentials.

'Welcome to Egypt,' he booms, and Abram remembers another booming voice, not so long ago, not welcoming him but sending him out, urging him to take a risk and give up real estate forever. Surely this isn't the distant land that ageless Spokesman had in mind.

'I've heard of you, Abram, you're famous – but I knew nothing of your family. There's not a face like this in all of Egypt. And I should know, I've studied them all very closely.'

His glistening cheeks are an inch from Sarai's now. She can smell the fish on his breath.

Abram summons his courage, steels himself for the moment he knew would come. With God on his side he can do this, with God on his side he can face anyone and be strong, with God on his side he can speak truth and act justly . . . with God on his side he can say,

'Sarai's my sister.'

One big fat whopping yellow lie.

Pharaoh's eyebrows raise a little. This is not the answer he was expecting.

'Really? I thought . . .'

'No, no, she's my sister. Aren't you . . . dear?'

Sarai turns slowly, so so slowly, and her almond eyes are on fire. That exquisite face is a bleak, hopeless mask. She opens her mouth but her mind is not engaged, her brain is flipping somersaults as she tries to keep up here. 'Yes,' she whispers. 'Whatever you say.'

Abram winces as he hears her. She gives nothing away but he knows her too well; the merest flicker of her eyes tells him everything. The betrayal may have saved his life, but something inside Sarai is about to die.

A week later and Abe's well in with the royal court. He spends his evenings jawing with the local big shots, putting the empire to rights and lamenting the troubles of the local camel bladder-ball team. They'll be out of the Premier League next season. And things looked so good when it all began. How could it turn so sour so quickly?

Three floors below things don't look so rosy for Sarai, either. Every night she tarts up with the other concubines. Three hours of polish and perfume, paint and powder. The king likes his women like oil paintings, flawless and uncomplaining as he satisfies his every royal whim. She's seen the other girls return from a night in his boudoir, sometimes they limp back, and inside they're always broken. It's rumoured that tonight will be her big night. You go girl – you give the king a night he'll never forget, you get to be the royal mattress for ten hours. What an honour. She's so stressed about the whole thing she's bitten her nails down to the quick and lately small patches of eczema have broken out all over her body. Still, that may prove to be an advantage if it turns the royal loins cold.

Sarai watches the palace eunuchs descend the golden steps into the harem and she bites her lip, putting a crack in her lip gloss. These half-men do the king's dirty work – they pick the women and line them up, making sure they're subservient and well-groomed. Horror stories abound about the girls who said 'No' to the royal appetite. Yet Sarai knows. She shouldn't be here. She's better than all this. She thought Abram was too. But now she wonders. As she sits and adjusts her braided skirts, she really wonders. Is he up there plotting to get her out? Is he pacing the floor and breaking his heart over his deceitful cowardice? Or is he playing cards and swapping stories about bladder-ball, enjoying his freedom and eyeing up the local girls? Perhaps he even has his eye on one of the other women from the harem, free and wandering about up there on a night off, three floors above her misery.

It takes four attempts to activate the central locking on my Ford Money-pit. My key is old and the rubber casing on it long perished. I get in, ignore my seatbelt, swerve out of the drive and head straight out of town. Past the kids' school, past the police station and the local supermarket, past Cutter's with all its history. Out, out into the stratosphere, well the ring road anyway, where I promptly get lost and drive endlessly round and round for a while. I don't know where I'm going, and I never intended to get in my car at all today.

My wife left half an hour ago with my wallet and our three kids for a long bank holiday weekend with her brother, his wife and their posse of little darlings. We barely said goodbye to each other, adopted forced smiles that looked more like gashes in a broken window, and then I watched while she struggled to force too many bags into too small a boot. I went out to help her but she snarled like a Rottweiler with PMT and when my wife's in that kind of mood, her bite is most definitely worse than her bark.

So, having three empty days I planned to use the time creatively – i.e. go back to bed and do nothing for seventy-two hours. Just lie there and watch the fast food cartons pile up round my chin. So why did I jump in the car with my one remaining credit card and a half-filled rucksack and take off like Abram into the sunrise? Well of course I'm running away, at least for a weekend. And of course I'll come back. But for three heady days I can take off and just drive, no destination, no deadline. Just journeying. Nowhere to go, no one to please, no one to entertain. Just me and my mile-wide selfish streak. Bliss.

Bliss, bliss, bliss.

What can you do with three days? What do you do when everything else falls away and for seventy-two hours it's as if your normal dull world doesn't exist? Anything can happen. You can be anyone. It's Groundhog Day – nothing has any consequences. You're James Bond, Indiana Jones, Vasco da Gama, Captain Scott, Tintin or, in my case, Johnny English. But I can still go anywhere and be anyone. So I drive. I drive past all the places that suddenly seem like little prisons to me. The workplace, the playgroup, the shops. And the church. Davey's on the road again and the years are falling away. I'm a rocketman on my way to Mars, I'm gonna go go go. Till I notice my petrol gauge is low and I have to stop for fuel. No worries. I put a tiger in the tank, air in the wheels and a ton of chocolate in the glove box. Yorkies of course, what else for the man who's left everything?

I get coffee too and a double chocolate doughnut, and for a few distracted minutes I have my first quiet time in months, slumped behind the wheel with the sound of juggernauts revving up inches from my left shoulder while a torrent of 4x4s thunder by on my right. I pull out my little black Bible and thumb through the tattered pages for someone else on a road trip. Abram, he'll do. Get on your camel, mate, and ride. Off into the unknown, forget your troubles and your mortgage, start doing some real living. Only with him it isn't just for a weekend – it's forever. No more cool evenings lounging in the back garden with a can of Jonah Smith's. No more trips down to B&Q for some new shelves and a bit of decking. You won't need that discount card any more Abe, you'll be in a tent for the rest of your puff. You'll see your life out under the stars from now on. When God promised this guy a future littered with bright lights, he really meant it. Abram spent every last one of his final days adjusting guy ropes and brewing up on a calor gas stove.

Maybe that's why Egypt seemed so appealing – perhaps reality was setting in and Abram was weary of life on the back of a camel. It wasn't the road trip he'd imagined. Sand for miles and no neighbours to invite round of an evening. And where was it all going to end anyway? The lot of them; nothing but a pile of clean white bones with a couple of frisky vultures crouching on top? Maybe Egypt held a new life. Maybe this was the land God had meant. It was suddenly full of a million bright lights, twinkling African stars that could offer Abe a promising future. Or maybe it really was just a pit stop, a pull-in to a convenient service station to pick up some fuel and fast food. Either way it all went very wrong. Like so many road movies, the happy couple knock on a stranger's door and encounter hell. Abe's left pacing the floor wondering at the audacity of his own cowardice, Sarai's stuck in the royal harem scratching off the days till it's her turn to jolly the royal loins. How the mighty fall. One minute he's the father of the faith, the next he's the father of lies. How could he have done it? How could he have started so well and ended so badly?

Just when you're on the up, a spectacular down comes along to remind you how human you really are.

Sometimes I'm most susceptible to the fall when I've just been flying higher than ever. But I don't want to think about that. I know that I could do an Abram, I know I can lie and turn tail, rip open my Superman costume to reveal yellow underwear, but I'm just beginning. I'm packing the camels and heading off into the unknown. It won't fall apart. I'll be careful. Whatever that means.

2. Blood and Guts

Judges 3:7–11

Joshua's body is still warm when the trouble begins. The breath has gone from his lungs and the sight has long left his eyes, but the heat still lingers in his chest as the leaders start squabbling for power. It's not long before bad turns to worse and Joshua's spinning like a roulette wheel in his newly dug grave.

Within days his burial plot lies in the shadow of a freshly formed idol. Bits of lifeless stone and wood shoot up all over the horizon, and the people who once followed a God who could move faster than lightning now bow down to effigies that can't even fall over without help.

Caleb's an old man on his last legs, but he can still do more than any carved image. Up in his home in the mountains he hears the stories and sighs. Up here, men still honour the living God, they worship the One who made wood and stone. Caleb leans on his staff and rubs his aching spine.

'I didn't fight for this,' he snarls, ' I didn't give up one life of slavery just so we could replace it with another. Why do they fall on their faces before these cartoon gods?'

Othniel sits nearby and sharpens a stick with his hunting knife.

'Because they have bad memories and short sight,' he says. 'They just react to whatever comes along. And now Josh's gone, they fear God's left too. They'll have any bit of deity they can find. You know what they say, uncle, when a man stops believing in something, he'll put his faith in anything.'

'If that's true then we're all in trouble. Dig a big hole and hide in it, Othniel, before they bury you in one, cos you can guarantee one thing – our enemies will be here like dogs, tearing our flesh and slaughtering our children quicker than you can say ethnic cleansing. You watch, without God we're nothing.'

Caleb spits in the dust and limps back inside. His saliva is yellow and shows vivid signs of his diminishing health. By the morning the breath will have left his body too. Fortunately he won't be around long enough to realise he's a darn good prophet.

Years pass. Conquerors come and go. People die and God's nation is abused and mutilated. Othniel never forgets that evening chat with his uncle, and it's not long before he feels a tap on his shoulder and a boot up the backside and he discovers the Spirit of the Lord is anointing him for more than just the weekly sermon slot. He dusts off his sword, polishes his shield and tries to inject some truth and courage into a thousand wayward soldiers.

Funny how lunch time always arrives three hours early when you're driving. Somehow that endless string of service stations just piles on the hunger. I stop at a Blissful Diner. I order more junk food than I've consumed all year and take stock. I left in such a rush that I neglected to pack properly – that was half the joy of leaving. No boot to stuff with tricycles, spare nappies, cool bags, glitter-speckled wellingtons, giant Mr

Miserable buckets and spades, pushchairs, deckchairs, highchairs, car seats and king-sized space hoppers. Just me, my old battered Bible, a packet of jaffa cakes, a couple of jumpers, some spare boxers and a toothbrush. Only I forgot the toothbrush. And the spare boxers.

But for now I forget all that and appreciate being in the middle of nowhere. I open my eyes, I mean really open them, look around at the lorry drivers and the green-capped motorway staff, the book reps and the football fans. Everyone's got their own little plastic table, their own tiny bit of Little Britain. Just like me. Marking out my territory. I may not be physically sitting in my favourite chair beside that roaring fire in Cutter's – but I am on the inside. You can take the bloke out of the pub – but you can't take the pub out of the bloke.

I smile and nod to myself, then see that I've been spotted smiling and nodding to myself by the teenager on the till and I do my utmost to make it look as if I was just coughing and trying to shake some wax out of my ear. Like that would really work.

I fill my mouth with so much fast food it'll take a very long time to eat it. So while I'm waiting I flip open my Bible and my eyes fall on Othniel, one of the many saviours in the book of Judges. Judges is full of sinning and saviours. The people get it wrong, everything falls apart, they get beaten up, they promise never to get it wrong again and God sends them a saviour. This happens time and again: Deborah, Ehud, Gideon . . . the list is endless and includes dear old Othniel, a chip off his uncle's block. It must have been hard standing in Caleb's shadow – especially as uncle Caleb was by then standing on his own mountain. Caleb was the Cliff Richard of Israel. The Mick Jagger who didn't believe in the ageing process. He just went on and on and on. But Othniel's been watching and learning and, now his uncle's gone, it's his turn. He ain't afraid to take a risk. He'll flush out the bad guys and kick some Canaanite buttocks.

Sometimes it seems as if people think the Bible is full of sweetness and light and H.E. Bates stories, instead of the real life that's jammed in those pages. It's more like an episode of *Cracker* or *Taggart*. Most of the sermons I hear present it as a book full of *right* answers, disregarding all the questions, doubts, fears and fury that you can actually encounter in there. The problem is, the people on those wafer thin pages are normal. They live through wars and famines, plague and violence, just as we do today. The Bible isn't set in Neverland. It's not a book of kids' stories, it's the accounts of bad people trying to follow a good God. His name isn't 'Eh oh!' it's 'I am.' It's not 'Yah boo!' it's 'Yahweh'. The Bible's life – not children's television.

Othniel doesn't get much press here. He's just one of that list of judges, maybe slightly under the thumb, as it's recorded his wife coerces him into demanding a bit of extra land at one point.

When the people feel the iron hand of King Cushan-Rishathaim of Aram-Naharaim (try saying that after a few brews of milk and honey) they, like me in a tight corner, promise God they'll behave from now on, and the ever-patient God of heaven hand-picks Othniel. Much hacking of limbs ensues, no doubt there's a lot of football played with enemy heads and before you can say King Cushan-whatshisface of Aram-whatever the people are free and spraying each other with bottles of Canaanite champagne. Othniel takes charge and there's peace in the land. Till the next time.

Some folk say the Old Testament's just about fighting. It's the reason they don't read it much. They say how can *that* God be a God of love? He just tells his mates to kill people all the time. Really? I'm not so sure. Firstly these folk probably imagine love to represent an old lady with pink slippers and a dressing gown cuddling the Andrex puppy whilst watching another lady in pink slippers and a dressing gown present *Songs of Praise*. Forget that for a game of Laser Quest. And secondly, it's a massive generalisation, somewhere about the size of the Empire State Building, to say that all of the Old Testament is about war. Sure there's a warring phase – mostly from the book of Judges through to 2 Chronicles; 2 Chronicles being the sequel to 1 Chronicles. Personally I'd have preferred a title like Chronicles Reloaded, or Chronicles Episode Two: Solomon Strikes Back.

But after that phase, well, seems to me the main message in there is about the little people – widows, orphans, strangers and outcasts and how to look after them. Burnt offerings, charred meat, smoking grain? You can keep it, lads. I'd rather have a bowl of kindness from you. A plate of justice mixed with a bowl of mercy with a tankard of humility to wash it all down, thanks. Bring me a load of that and I'll be well-chuffed. Singing songs and setting light to furry creatures is all well and good – but it's you I want on the altar 24/7.

And while we're on the subject – what's worship anyway? For years I never bothered to ask the question.

'Right, I see. So I just stand in this row and sing lots of old songs I don't understand and lots of new ones that don't make much sense. Okay. And then I act like I'm at school and stand and sit and nod and listen to a lesson. Okay. Fine. Cos that's the way Jesus did it, wasn't it? Wasn't it?'

How does creation praise its designer? By doing what it was designed to do, doing what it does best. Thundering, showering, snowing, dawning, budding, changing and growing. Worship is not a jumper we put on once a week to cover the shabby bits of the rest of our lives; it's a sigh that we express, every single day. It comes out of us naturally. Doing what we do, living as we live, rich and poor, good moods and bad. And when we each do what we've been designed to do best – whatever talents we have – that's the clearest expression of praise in our repertoire.

Othniel did what he did best. He rescued a nation and brought peace to the land. That's worship.

Excuse me while I just put my soapbox away. It's a flatpack from IKEA.

3. The Good Book Just Got Better

Genesis 1 to Malachi 4
(It might take you a while)

I thought I might get a paper but there's clearly no news today. The headlines trumpet the fact that the male sperm count is down and the female word count is up. Apparently it's official now, women are wired to deliver thirteen thousand more words a day than each man. Thirteen thousand! How do they find the energy?

So whilst waiting for my healthy alternative of double sausages, eggs, black pudding, burgers, bacon, mushrooms and deep fried bread to digest, I take time to reflect on this small but much-maligned good book. I grab a stained serviette and scribble down my easy-read version of the Old Testament. A sort of good book you can read in seven and a half minutes.

> Okay. So the start is straightforward, everyone knows about the big bang and the slugs that crept out of the sea, put on clothes and turned into people. Only kidding. I know all about creation, honest. It was all jotted down by Moses. In fact the first few books of the Bible were all jotted down by Moses.
>
> You could say they were the very first trilogy – except that there were five of them. But enough waffle, let's cut to the chase.

In Genesis God took some space to make a perfect world, then Adam and Eve took some fruit and made it crumble. So God made the first car and drove them out of the garden. Noah shaped an Ark and Joseph became a musical.

In Exodus there was a burning bush, plagues in Egypt and the Ten Commandments.

The rules arrived on tablets of stone and Moses cracked the first lot, so God carved some more – and nobody's cracked them since.

Leviticus is rather like an episode of *Morse* – it's all about the law and it takes forever.

The book of Numbers contains an awful lot of er . . . numbers.

Deuteronomy was the first sermon. It went on for quite a while. No change there then.

The next twelve books are hysterical. Sorry, historical.

Joshua was rather big on dairy products, his book contains walls of Jericho, lions of Judah and the land of milk and honey. Oh and a lot of disappointed Canaanites.

Judges is a gentle book containing sex, violence, rape, massacre, brutality and deceit.

While Ruth is a swashbuckling action-adventure-murder-mystery – without the action, adventure, murder or mystery.

Oh and nobody swashes their buckles either.

In Samuel 1 Hannah became a mother, Samuel became a mystic, David became a musician and Saul became mad.

Hannah bore Samuel, Samuel bore divine messages, David bored a hole in Goliath's head and Saul bored everybody.

This adventure was closely followed by Samuel 2 – The shepherd strikes back.

In which David plays the King and becomes a liar. I'm sorry! David plays the lyre and becomes a King.

He ushered in a golden age of peace, prosperity and peeking through other people's bedroom windows.

First Kings featured . . . the first kings. And a dubious lot they were.

Dysfunctional families, wayward children and duplicitous servants. Nothing changes, does it?

Kings 2 was the sequel – what you might call the Return of the Kings. It starred Elisha the prophet, not to be confused with Elijah the prophet. And just to clear this up once and for all – Elijah is the one who built the mother of all bonfires, dined out with the ravens and went to heaven in a chariot of fire. Or was that Elisha? No – Elisha was the one who raised the dead, savaged forty-two young men with a couple of wild bears, and did a posthumous miracle. Or was that Elijah?

Chronicles 1 is a sort of remake of Kings – and let's face it – they're never as good as the originals, are they?

In Chronicles: Reloaded, David's son Solomon built a magnificent Temple and got married in it . . . seven hundred times.

But time and polygamy took its toll and by the book of Ezra the people of Israel were all in Exile. I think that's somewhere between Exeter and Exmouth.

Nehemiah's book is a sort of Jewish version of *Ground Force*. He mobilised a small team to rebuild the walls of Jerusalem while the residents were out for the weekend.

He enlisted the help of Bob the Bethlehem stonemason and Lala, Dipsy and Po the Tel Aviv Tubbies.

Esther is a tragedy of Shakespearean proportions. It includes genocide, anti-Semitism and a beauty pageant. In a nutshell, Zeresh is married to Haman, Haman hates Mordecai, Mordecai adores Esther, Esther marries

Xerxes, Xerxes divorces Vashti, Vashti loves herself and they don't all live happily ever after.

Then came the books of wisdom – containing songs, sketches and jokes old and new.

Tucked away somewhere between the pain, depression and rather nasty skin diseases.

The first book is that of Job. It features Job, Job's comforters and Job's medical problems.

Psalms is King David's private journal – he still doesn't realise it's been published around the globe and read by all and sundry.

In Proverbs diamonds aren't a girl's best friend, one in the eye is not worth two in the ear, there are no instructions regarding having cake and eating it and there's no mention of getting stoned in glass houses. It is, in fact, King Solomon's private journal and he still doesn't realise it's been published around the globe and read by no one at all.

Ecclesiastes is Solomon's guide to achieving money, sex and power.

In his words – been there, done that, got the loincloth.

Song of Songs is an erotic love poem *and it's in the Bible!*

Honest! It's written by Solomon and he should know what he's talking about – he had more honeymoons than Henry VIII!

Goodness knows when he found the time to write so many books. Check out the pomegranates . . .

And then came the prophets – imagine if you will a mixed bag of weird people with strange clothes and unusual habits. Or just pop down to your local church.

Isaiah was an eloquent orator. He compiled sixty-six chapters writ large with deep waters and raging fires, eagles' wings and mourning doves, gentle lions and roaring lambs. Oh and he went round butt-naked for a while.

Jeremiah is just downright depressing. He told tales of slavery, suffering and sour grapes. He didn't get invited to many parties.

In Lamentations, the writer gets beaten up. Bears, lions, soldiers, ostriches and wine merchants all conspire against him. The writer's name is Jeremiah. Now there's a surprise.

Ezekiel was the first mime artist. Instead of shouting in the street, he gesticulated in the gutter. A sort of spiritual charades. His most famous shows included *Shaving in Public*, *Cooking with Cow Dung* and the musical comedy *Dem Bones, Dem Bones, Dem Dry Bones*.

In Daniel, our eponymous hero escapes death by fire, death by lions, death by mad kings and death by chocolate.

The book of Hosea is a tragic tale of spurned love and lost innocence. It's not so much about vicars and tarts as prophets and prostitutes.

Joel whizzes by in a flash of rumbling chariots, forest fires, marauding armies and cataclysmic earthquakes. But it's not all good news – this is the biblical book where locusts big it up. There are hopping locusts, cutting locusts, swarming locusts and stripping locusts. (Not to be confused with lap-dancing locusts.)

Moving swiftly on, Amos was a farmer, a rough and ready lad who gave up ploughing his fields and scattering in order to speak of plumb lines, ripe fruit, fresh grain and – of course – more locusts.

Obadiah wasn't one of the four Yorkshiremen – he was Judean. His book has one chapter . . . and in his day there were thirty-four prophets living in t'shoebox in middle o't' road. They had it tough. But no locusts.

In his book Jonah gets a mission from God, gets depressed, gets on a boat, gets thrown into the sea, gets swallowed by a fish, gets depressed, gets vomited, gets evangelistic, gets depressed, gets sunburnt and gets depressed. Just another boring Monday then.

Micah foresaw many awesome and fearful things – but only one of his visions became a popular Christmas song. I'm referring to *O Little Town of Bethlehem* – not *Frosty the Snowman*.

Nahum arrives with good news and bad news for the city of Nineveh. The bad news is they're soon to be totally annihilated. The good news is there are a lot of cheap holidays on offer to Nineveh that year.

Habakkuk complained to God and climbed a watchtower. The fig trees hadn't blossomed and there were no grapes on the vines. The olive crop had failed, the flocks died in the field and the cattle barns were empty. And the bin men hadn't taken all his rubbish away *yet again*. No wonder he was so fed up. Yet he went on to say, 'Nevertheless, I will praise the Lord . . .'

Zephaniah spoke of a day of darkness. A day of black storm clouds. A day when noon will be as dark as night. A sort of typical August bank holiday Monday.

Haggai told people off for looking after number one and forgetting the important things in life. We really took a lot of notice of that message, didn't we?

Zechariah saw a woman in a basket, four blacksmiths, a man with a tape measure and a flying book. He struggled to understand why so few took him seriously.

And finally Malachi brought some good news. A new day is coming, a day when calves will leap for joy, a day when the windows of heaven will be thrown wide and goodness will rain down. A day of hope, a day without spin doctors and stress, diets and keys, a day without political correctness, mobile phones and undercooked sprouts.

And then everything went very quiet for four hundred years . . . too quiet.

So you see – the Old Testament is full of plenty more than just violence. The *battling* years gave way to the *being beaten up* years, which gave way to the *building* years, which gave way to more *being beaten up* years. Once Chronicles: Reloaded ends there's very little opportunity to accuse God of *telling the Israelites to punch the lights out of their neighbours*. And even when they had the power, much of the time the people abused it with no divine licence whatsoever. In their heyday, when the word on the sand was 'Don't mess with them Joshua-types', it seems to me God does his best to try and work with them as a warring nation. Once they become a '*Quick! Run away!*' nation, he adjusts and works with that. They hang up their swords and pick up their lyres and start bashing on about the Rivers of Babylon.

I flip to Isaiah and find plenty of references about inviting the world to a party rather than a punch-up. Everyone's invited. Especially the lowlife. There's plenty of good news in there if you look.

But I have to say I do need these tales of derring-do. I don't want just happy stories of repentant lambs and persistent widows. I need the biblical Jack Sparrows. I need all that swashing and buckling; all those storms and monsters that Job and John face in their widescreen encounters with the Almighty. Primroses and sunsets don't hit the spot. They don't push my buttons. I want more. And my guess is – so do all these other guys I'm not sharing my lunch with, the reps, the fans, the green-capped teenagers. They don't want *do this, do that, thou shalt and thou shan't and thou shouldn't* . . . They want what Jesus gave 'em – tales of the unexpected. Action adventure; stories of mayhem and murder, twists and turns, heroes and villains, blood and guts. Never mind Paul and his *Love is* poetry. Give us the hard stuff. The words of wisdom are still all in there, woven through the sex and violence, writ large in the blood and sand – I want to be able to work it out for myself, and I'd rather do it whilst watching some gladiators and bravehearts slice big bits off each other.

4. Snog of Snogs

Songs of Songs 1:1–4; 7:1–9

This is Solomon's Song of Songs, more wonderful than any other.

> *Young Woman:* 'Kiss me again and again, for your love is sweeter than wine. How fragrant your cologne, and how pleasing your name! No wonder all the young women love you! Take me with you. Come, let's run! Bring me into your bedroom, O my king.'
>
> *Young Man:* 'How beautiful are your sandalled feet, O queenly maiden. Your rounded thighs are like jewels, the work of a skilled craftsman. Your navel is as delicious as a goblet filled with wine. Your belly is lovely, like a heap of wheat set about with lilies. Your breasts are like twin fawns of a gazelle. Your neck is as stately as an ivory tower. Your eyes are like the sparkling pools in Heshbon by the gate of Bath-rabbim. Your nose is as fine as the tower of Lebanon overlooking Damascus. Your head is as majestic as Mount Carmel, and the sheen of your hair radiates royalty. A king is held captive in your queenly tresses.
>
> Oh, how delightful you are, my beloved; how pleasant for utter delight! You are tall and slim like a palm tree, and your breasts are like its clusters of dates. I said, 'I will climb up into the palm tree and take hold of its

branches. Now may your breasts be like grape clusters,
and the scent of your breath like apples. May your
kisses be as exciting as the best wine, smooth and sweet,
flowing gently over lips and teeth.'

It's raining. The water's bouncing off the windows like
hard globs of wax. I finish up my fried elevenses and
head for the shop. I don't need anything but I'm on a
journey – I have to buy crisps, chocolate, a film magazine, a muffin and a road map. Plus three CDs of music
I've not heard for twenty years. The kind of music that
made my youth what it was. Goodness knows why I
should want to revisit it.

I'm innocently looking for a copy of *The Best Film
Magazine in the World* and instead find myself gazing up
at a series of naked torsos. How did that happen?
Suddenly I'm standing in front of a rack *Loaded* with
Stuff that appeals to my *Nuts* and rouses the kind of animal instincts that belong in a zoo, not a motorway service station. My first instinct is to glance around and
make sure no one else has noticed. The two girls behind
the counter are chatting to each other and doing their
best to ignore any passing customers. We English have
perfected the art of taking people's money without making eye contact.

Recently my wife and I ploughed through the racks of
a stand just like this one. Fervently inspired, I had sug-
gested trying to find a lad's mag that didn't have bra-
less women on every other page. My wife offered to flip
through and tear out all the naked babes – and I then
considered making a calendar out of the extracted pictures (brilliant – twelve birds with one stone). There we
were just standing in Tescos, both of us closely examin-
ing technicolour glossy pics in a publication dedicated
to football, firearms and foreplay, a sort of booters,

shooters and hooters thing, when two friends appeared from nowhere with innocent smiles and raised eyebrows. I of course played it cool, turned crimson and pretended we do that sort of thing every week. Don't you just love it when that happens? Life has this glorious way of ambushing you.

Okay so what is this Song of Songs all about? Beautiful people with breasts like fresh fruit, thighs like sleek stones and kisses like Irish whiskey. Can this really be on the pages of my good book? Tucked between the world-weary wrath of Jeremiah and the poetic prophecy of Isaiah? It's like suddenly coming across *Confessions of a Window Cleaner* wedged tightly between *Chariots of Fire* and *Schindler's List*. Somebody's made a grave error here. Where were the theology police on the day they let King Solomon's Mind run rampant across the pages of this sacred scroll?

Some bloke in a dog collar with snowstorm dandruff and way too much nasal hair will assure you it's all some great metaphor about Jesus loving people – but I can't see it myself – I'm not convinced. If God made sex he made sex, and we may be embarrassed about two people getting loved up but you can bet an actress to a bishop that he sure ain't.

So is Song of Songs the page 3 of the good book? Might as well be for all the time we spend studying it in church.

I mean come on, a bloke with seven hundred wives and concubines writes an intercourse like this – it's gotta be about sex, surely? So that said – is it *Mills and Boon* or *Men Only?*

Well . . . neither. The sex is too reverent for locker room chat, but not cheesy enough for your romance monthly. It's poetic – you'll find herds of gazelles and fields of pomegranates where there should be a centrefold pin-up.

The language is frank but full of respect. These two young lovers are working hard to tell each other to jump in and get lost in the undiscovered countries of each other's bodies. And they're not the only ones. Other women encourage them on! (Where are the other men? Presumably out in a back room somewhere poring over a copy of Songs of Songs uncut – the version they tried to ban.)

But the girls are in the stands chanting, 'Go on, my son!' 'Get in there, girl!' 'Ay o . . . ay o, ay o, ay o!'

It's like a cross between Cup Final night and *Blind Date*. But there's little room for shame or embarrassment. In fact, no room at all. Propriety, what's that? Two people in love, get down, get with it. Make the most of it, get those sky rockets in flight, get on with that afternoon delight. Sex in here is a verb, not a gender description.

Does it turn me on? Well, frankly yes. But many things do that, and it's no crime to be stimulated by the thought of two lovers giving pleasure to each other. If some folk had their way, you'd never look at a pair of coconuts or a gherkin just in case it inspired fire in your loins.

I guess if God had been shy he wouldn't have invented sex. And it seems he made it deliberately comical too. As a friend of mine says, it's all about belching, squelching and farting. The bump and grind of cool pop songs is actually much more like huff and puff.

And speaking of songs, the obvious problem with Solomon's unplugged ballads of course is that they're supposed to be sung. Reading this stuff is a bit like studying the CD sleeve instead of listening to the album. Same with the Psalms too. They need a backing track. *Hey Jude* and *Smells Like Teen Spirit* probably wouldn't be the timeless classics they are, had John, Paul and Kurt not thought to add their little ditties to those legendary lyrics. The same could be said of so many rap classics – oh no, I'm sorry – there are no rap classics. Which just proves the point: King Solomon and DJ Tuneless need to get themselves a melody.

Mind you – can you imagine singing *Your breasts are like twin fawns – a cluster of ripe figs* to the tune of *Morning Has Broken*? It might happen . . .

This stuff we avoid in church is actually celebrated in fine style right here in this story of God. And maybe that's the point – sex hidden away is the kind of sex that destroys us. Sex discussed and laughed about might fill the room with red faces – but it's a lot more healthy that way.

I leave the pouting glossy magazine girls and saunter off with a great big grin on my face, which probably doesn't look good at all. But who cares? If Solomon can smile at sex, so can I.

5. Paraders of the Lost Ark

2 Samuel 6:1–23

David's on an up. Not always the case with this bi-polar king. This rocker warrior has had his fair share of peaks and troughs. His bulging book of poems tells the tall tales and sad stories; those days of dank despair and nights of black moods. The darkness has often threatened to swallow him alive. But not today, today his mind is a fairground attraction, all bright lights and candy floss.

This is a moment he's dreamt of since he was a kid. Success, fame, glory – he's got it all. And to top it off – it's all for God.

Michal sighs and wrestles the brush through her rampant wild hair. It's always been rebellious and unrestrained, not unlike her heart. Always wild, always out of control. Like that first time she saw David and fell in love. She fell so easily, like a mountain of precariously stacked linen ephods. She and her brother first bumped into David as he played his harp to soothe the royal nerves in her father's tent. She handed over her heart there and then, and before long there was talk of a royal wedding. It was her dream come true.

But the truth was different. The whole thing was a set-up, a sham. She was nothing more than a prize, a bargaining chip. She adored this young musician, but her father manhandled that adoration. Packaged it and handed it to David as bait. Saul wanted David for dead meat. The intention was a funeral, not a wedding. So the gauntlet was laid down. Kill and mutilate a hundred Philistines and you can have my daughter. Oh great, so Michal's worth a hundred foreskins then. That really made her feel special. But back then she didn't care, she could swallow her pride, David loved her. That was enough. He was young, good looking, romantic, danger-ous. Back then she'd have put the Philistine body parts in a pie and cooked them for him if he asked. She'd have done anything. And she did do most things, including saving his life. There they were in bed one night, getting down to it, limbs and lips clamped together, when sud-denly smack! The front door caves in and an axe flies into the bedroom and embeds itself in the wall right beside her head. 'Quick Dave, out of the window, now! Now! Forget your clothes! Stop doing that! Run!'

So he jumped and ran, like a man possessed, naked and directionless through the night. And she didn't hear from him again. No word, no hastily scribbled message, no breathless servant arriving wet and half dead to tell her David's still out there pining for her. He just ups and dumps her. And dear old daddy decides she can do for some other bloke now. A quick convenient wedding and that's that. She couldn't complain, wouldn't want to, she had a good life with Palti. He certainly loved her, and maybe he kindled something similar in her own reckless heart. But her mind was always away somewhere else, running and hiding with David. Alive or dead, she wasn't going to give up on him.

Now here she is watching him leap about all over again, naked and directionless. Only this time he's king, and he's not running for his life, he's celebrating his great-ness. Well done, your Majesty. Well done. She leans on the window frame and watches him make a right idiot of himself. If only she could throw him out of a window now. What is he doing? Why's he out there without his clothes on? He used to be her hero – now he's horrible.

'David's the best man you'll ever meet,' her brother told her the day she first met him.

Jonathan held her gaze and his eyes burned it into her soul. 'There's no one like David. He has courage, wit, style and his heart is God's.'

Maybe that's the problem. Maybe if his heart had been hers she wouldn't be up here now nursing bitter memories. Maybe if his heart had been a bit lower than the heavens her brother would still be alive. It's all very well loving a God you can't see, but what about a wife you look at every day?

In the street David's hurling himself around like a tornado. His body spins and twitches like a break-dancer on speed. But not his mind – that's focused. Behind the twisting and shouting he's watching every move the crowd make. He doesn't want another fatal mistake. Twelve weeks back he got all excited about bringing home the godly prize, the lost Ark, so excited that he forgot the correct protocol and a man was struck dead. He won't make that mistake again. He's had time to think and check out the history. Today the appropriate people carry the Ark of the Covenant, and whenever possible they're making sacrifices. There's more spilt blood out there than that time he met the Philistine giant.

He wants to get this right, this moment is for God, it's the most important day of his life.

This is the hour he was born for, this is the time of his life, this is the cream on the . . .

'What the hell d'you think you're doing?'

Michal's standing there before him, her arms crossed, her face like flint, her hair wild and raging like a torrent of black sea.

'Don't talk to me like that. Especially not today.'

'Oh of course, this great and glorious day, oh flawless king.'

'Don't do this, Michal, not here, not now.'

The trumpets and singing are grinding to a precarious halt. A few brassy notes dribble into silence and the voices trickle away into awkward coughs. Embarrassment hangs in the air like a smell from the sewer.

David grits his teeth. 'The people are watching,' he snarls.

'Well I thought you'd already embarrassed yourself plenty, I can hardly add to that.'

'What are you talking about?'

'What am I talking about? Look, where are your clothes? There are single girls here. They don't want to see what you've got.'

'They're not looking at me, they have their eyes on God.'

Michal snorts and doesn't bother concealing a cynical smile. 'Oh right, of course. This is God's day. That's why you're the star of the show.'

'I am not. Michal – go home, we'll talk later.'

'Really? Well, that'll be a first. Talk later? We never talk later. That's always been your problem. You make empty promises to me. You never bring me in to your life. You've never involved me in one single decision that mattered. I loved you, David. I loved you. You just love your God and yourself.'

'Why shouldn't I? God chose me over your father, over your family.'

Michal stares at him. He's never spoken like this. He's always refused to dishonour her dad. What's become of him? When did he become this spiritual zombie?

'You've executed people for talk like that,' she shakes her head. 'What did I ever see in you?'

'Listen Michal . . .'

David's voice softens as he suddenly sees her pain. But she's turning away. He reaches out for her shoulder and spins her round.

'Listen! You're wrong about me, you're wrong about these girls. This day is for God, and if I look stupid then it's because he should be honoured and I shouldn't. I didn't ask for you to be treated the way you were. Your father brought that on. He gave you away to me, then he gave you to . . .'

David clutches at straws in his mind. He snaps his fingers and grimaces but the name won't come.

'You can't even remember his name, can you? The man I married, the man who loved me?'

'I'm the man you married, I loved you . . .'

'You had a funny way of showing it.'

She turns away again and this time she's too quick for his flailing hand.

He stands there yelling after her.

'God appointed me to do this. I'll do it the way he wants it. I will honour him – not you. He gave me these people to lead and to serve.'

She takes a final moment to pause and answer back.

'Then go ahead and serve them – you gave up serving me long ago.'

I have bought so much stuff in the motorway shop they give me a free bag for it all, not a bad deal for the fifty quid I've just spent. I use the bag and its contents as an umbrella and make for the car. The key still doesn't work properly so I stand there getting wet for a while as I wait for the technology to kick in.

Inside the car I sling the bag on the passenger seat and stare into the middle distance. Was it such a good idea to run away today? My wife and kids will be nearly there now. Nearly at that cottage in the Midlands. There'll be a fire in the grate, toys for the kids and tea on the hob for my wife. I suddenly get a vision of warm yellow lights twinkling from those bright cottage windows. Why did we have to part on such a sour note? Why were we arguing anyway? We've argued about a lot of things lately. The washing up, the tidying up, the missing pages from the *Radio Times*, the toothpaste all over the sink, the chocolate-spread sandwiches jammed in the drawer of the DVD player. That missing CD I found in the toilet cistern, that Kit Kat last seen under the duvet. All the important things in life. Politics and religion? Huh, we laugh at such trivialities. We argue about the tough issues – who last filled up the car, who last filled up the kettle. Who won the last argument and who started the current one. Solving Middle Eastern politics is a doddle compared to the complexities of our family life.

I put the key in the ignition and drive for a while. The windscreen wipers squeak badly, like a dozen mice in labour. They don't really deal with the rain either, just smear the water about on the screen like the visuals to an old *Doctor Who* intro. Blurred traffic signs fly by and passing lorries hurl dirty water over my side windows. Suddenly the road doesn't seem to be rising before me, the way ahead doesn't lead to the stars any more. The weather's turning malignant and if I'm not careful I'm gonna slip off the road and spend the weekend in the gutter.

Before I know it I've pulled over again and I'm flipping through my Bible in a lay-by. The rain's getting heavy and drumming intermittently on the roof, divine fingers tapping on the shoulder of my soul. I find myself staring at the account of poor Michal. The woman scorned who wasn't allowed her moment of fury. Marriage just ain't easy, is it? The family that prays together stays together. Yea, right. No one mentions the bloomin' hard work that it also takes, the putting up with stuff, and the overlooking of the same irritating behavioural patterns that occur again and again and again. What was that song Freddie Mercury sang on that glorious album released just before his death? Oh yea – *I can't live with you, I can't live without you.* Sometimes marriage feels like trying to mix oil and water, fire and ice, Sean Bean and Mr Bean, Tony Benn and Tony Blair, someone who loves Marmite with well . . . me. Which is actually very appropriate, cos my wife loves Marmite. I'm convinced Jesus never touched the stuff. If manna falls from heaven, Marmite bubbles up from hell.

I read recently that every married couple hits rock bottom sooner or later. The honeymoon really does end, the gloss chips off, the champagne loses its sparkle, the girl of your dreams turns into the devil woman. The soufflé hits the fan and all you can do is duck and get out the bottle of Jif. Doesn't matter whether you married Britney, Whitney, Scarlett or Charlotte. Sooner or later you're gonna roll over in bed and wonder why you didn't pick one of the others. She can be the most beautiful babe in the world but still look tarnished compared to the girl next door. You can't stay in love forever, despite the advice of Westlife, *Cosmopolitan*, Oprah or Richard Curtis. Sooner or later the wind beneath your wings fizzles to that brawling over breakfast. Life happens. There's nothing you can do, except knuckle down, face the music and roll with the punches. Which is why I'm running away. I guess if I'm honest this little foray into Prodigalville has been brewing for a while. The mountain of washing up, dirty nappies, recycled Coke bottles and dirty shoes has finally made me flip. I want time out, I want a space where I can listen to music which doesn't feature Noddy, Lala and the Lion King. A forgotten land where going for a ten-minute walk doesn't involve twenty minutes of coat-putting-on preparation time. A nirvana where you can lie in instead of being lied on. Surely that place must still be out there somewhere – even if it's only here in my car.

I seek solace in the book which deals with all tough subjects. My little battered Bible pulls no punches and spares no blushes. Firmly embedded in Samuel's twin bestsellers there's the torrid tale of David and his first missus.

The romance between the two of them gets going big time when she's handed over like a bag of money, literally a payment for one hundred flaps of Philistine skin. But they're young and in love, and like so many of us, they think nothing can tarnish true affection. They'll be together forever, nothing can come between them. Not even attempted murder, bigamy and a thousand miles. Then one night death comes knocking and she has to throw him from a window and start lying. Absence may make Michal's heart grow fonder, but it's not too long before being out of David's sight means being out of David's mind. He marries another girl, no two more, no three, four, five . . . Has a fistful of adventures and doesn't write home.

Michal proves useful to her father yet again – 'Don't worry about David, dear,' Saul says comfortingly, 'he's probably dead anyway, here, have a new husband. This one'll do. He's perfect for you – he doesn't want my job.'

So she starts a new life – and at least her new man shows his love by coming home every night. That is until her first love swaggers back – then her new man finds he has no home to come back to.

Who knows how Michal felt by then – elated that the man of her dreams still wanted her? Or torn between two lovers? Palti's so besotted he'll make a public idiot of himself, David's so distracted he just sees Michal as a useful pawn in a game of one-upmanship. Let's face it, he now has enough wives for one each day of the week – with a handy day of rest on the seventh when he can be a bachelor boy again. When he first loved Michal she was the one and only, now she's Ms Wednesday.

Michal's had a hard life. There's no denying that – and if David's got one fault, he's got a thousand. Maybe his worst is his naïve nature, or maybe he's a control freak. Either way a quick combing of the annals of his life shows that he wasn't one for keeping his family informed. There are no scenes featuring the wives and kids gathered in the drawing room with dad sat astride a bean bag debating whether they have Christmas at his parents or hers this year. David's a one-man band, a typical red-blooded loner: one hundred per cent first-class male. Goes off into his cave to make the big decisions of his life, then lets the family find out for themselves. Probably via the headlines on the ten o'clock news. He and Michal of course have history and it's about as bad as Charles and Diana. So is it all forgivable, her dramatic outburst on the day David returns with the lost Ark? Is it all perfectly acceptable behavior for an estranged princess?

No doubt nowadays Michal would have been given her own interview with Trevor McDonald, proclaiming her desire to be the queen of Israeli hearts. Probably a spot on Oprah and Trisha too. A *My husband's a cheating monarch!* special. I guess it all depends on your perspective. If you're the injured party, suffering from a married lifetime of being kept in the dark and never being sure when your partner will come home next – then yes, there's a case to answer here.

On the other hand, if you're a first-class male who likes to go off into his own cave, make all the major decisions alone no matter who they affect, and then take off on your own when your personal life backfires on you – well, hi there, d'you wanna be in my gang? There's always room for one more.

6. Cain Invents Homicide

Genesis 4:1–17

It ain't easy being the older brother. For one thing you can spend your life resenting your younger siblings. Things had been fine as long as Cain had been an only child. Two doting parents to wait on his every need, come running whenever he screamed, or faked a scream. A father with no real day job to speak of, a mother who thought he was the most beautiful child on the planet. Probably because he was the only child on the planet. But not for long. Sometime, when he was around the age of four or five, Adam and Eve brought forth more fruit from their loins. Then bang! Suddenly he's second best. Suddenly he's the second most beautiful kid in the universe.

'Abel needs more of our attention now, Cain. He's a lot younger than you, and you're a big boy now. Time to act your shoe size, not your age.'

So Cain became a loner. Left mum and dad to breast-feeding and changing fig leaves and wandered off to play with lion cubs and jackal pups. Harmless fun. He made friends of the four-legged variety and collected toads, newts, lizards and geckos. Well, it was no good trying to find the kid next door. There was no next door.

He occasionally meandered across the plain towards the big house on the prairie. But he always turned back before he got half way. Morbid curiosity drew him towards the house of God, but fear and the heat from the flaming six-winged seraphim always drove him back. It was just too scary for a little kid. The Creator of all things living in his thirty-six bedroomed holiday home with the four horsemen patrolling the gates astride their red, brown and grey stallions; flaming swords hanging by their sides and with eyes that could melt granite. Adam and Eve often went over of an evening, and one of the cherub cadets would crouch on a rock and baby-sit the kids. The next day the breakfast table would always be full of jaw-dropping tales of awe and wonder, about riding unicorns over grand canyons and arm-wrestling minotaurs in some distant labyrinth. But Cain wasn't the adventurous type, and a story he once heard about a mythical sly serpent in a far-off loch put him off searching for too many weird creatures. They said this monster could suck the life out of you just by looking into your eyes, and his mother shuddered whenever the word 'serpent' crept into the conversation. So Cain steered clear of the big house on the prairie and little by little, day by day, he grew up in the shadow of his younger brother. Abel on the other hand often ventured across the plain. He seemed to have no fear of fire or pale riders. And the more he grew in confidence, the more Cain resented it.

'The Boss wants us to take over some of our stuff.'

Abel squinted at his brother as he took the lamb's leg and snapped it cleanly. He pulled the bleating creature from the claws of the hedge and threw it astride his shoulders.

'He won't run off again in a hurry.'

Cain winced. He winced every time he heard the crack of a little animal's foreleg snapping in his brother's calloused hands.

'Have to do it,' Abel breezed. 'They have to learn I'm the shepherd. Can't have 'em running off a cliff, or getting lost and eaten by the minotaur.'

'No one's ever seen the minotaur eat one of your lambs.'

'All right, the loch serpent then.'

'Or the loch serpent, and the chances are that's just a myth anyway.'

'Look, this is off the point. The Boss has asked us to go and see him. And take over some of our work.'

'He's not *the Boss* – he's God. You're too familiar with him.'

'How would you know – you never go see him. He might be called Blastus for all you know.'

'Blastus? That's not a name.'

'It is.'

Cain sighed. His brother always out-talks him, always has an answer, always goes on about *the Boss*.

'You should get to know him better, Cain. You'd love him.'

'No I wouldn't. He frightens me, he's too big.'

'How would you know? Actually he's only three foot four.'

'Is he?'

Abel shrugged. 'You'll soon find out. I said we'd be over tomorrow night. Bring some of those weeds you're always growing. I'll take a new lamb.'

'Well, don't break its legs.'

'Too late. I did yesterday.'

Cain hated his brother's barbaric attitude. Cain always loved the creatures: the beasts, birds, fish, insects. All of 'em. His favourite bedtime story was always his father's epic *Naming of the animals*.

Cain turns up with a sack full of goodies. Abel's standing beside a young fig tree. Everything's young round here, everything still smells new and clean, like it's just come out of the shop. There's no newborn lamb though. No sound of bleating.

'Where's yours?' asks Cain, looking all around him.

Abel holds up a bag made of stitched leaves.

'You're kidding!'

'No. I took the best bits from it.'

'You killed it?'

'Oh no. It's still all moving around in here like a cute, woolly jigsaw – I'm hoping to put it back together again afterwards . . . Course I killed it, you bozo.'

Cain spits at the ground beside his brother's foot. 'Parrot snake!' he hisses.

Abel raises his eyebrows but he's not fussed.

'Come on, the Boss is waiting.'

Cain feels himself tighten up as they walk across the plain. He's never conquered this fear and he's never likely to. Abel, on the other hand, saunters beside him, kicking at rocks and hurling stray clods of earth at nearby meerkats.

'Made up another song yesterday,' he says.

Cain grunts. His brother's always making up songs; but if you can't kick it, stroke it or build something out of it, Cain's not interested.

'Can't quite get the last line. listen: *There's nothing you can swing that can't be swung, nothing you can't fling that can't be flung, no neck you can't wring that can't be wrung, it's easy. All you need is . . .*'

He grimaces at his brother. Cain grimaces back then says, his voice cold as ice,

'*A big black pus-filled heart.*'

Abel frowns then says, 'No, won't scan.' He thinks. 'I like the idea of singing about hearts though. *Don't go busting my heart.* That might make a good line.'

'How about *Don't go busting my leg*? You could dedicate it to all your favourite lambs as they hobble about.'

They walk on in silence. There are days when Abel just does not get his brother. As they near the house, and the shadow of that huge luminous building falls across them both, Abel mutters,

'Dad says we need a couple of wives.'

'What? Like – women?'

'Yea.'

'Where from?'

'He says we should ask the Boss about that one.'

They nod at the flaming seraphim as they pass between the gates: Abel out of familiarity, Cain out of fear. Nearby, a pale horse thunders towards them from the direction of the stables; its rider gleaming white and the size of Cain and his brother put together. The horse pulls up and the rider says something to Abel in a strange language. Abel replies and they go on in.

'How d'you know what he says?'

'The Boss gives lessons – well, Michael does.'

'Michael? Who's Michael?' . . .

Cain stands breathless and bloody now. His fists look like dead animals – all caked in mud and bodily fluids. He's never noticed how big they are before; he has hands like a jackal's head. He wipes them down his shirt and smears the incriminating mixture across him. He'd sometimes wondered how long it might take to end a life. Less than five minutes is his answer. He waited for Abel beside the waterhole, crouching in the shadow of a boulder. Then, as he heard the footsteps crunching closer, he leapt out from his hunched position and grabbed Abel's neck with his pincer fingers. The force from that strike alone must have done a lot of the damage, the two of them crashing backwards onto the hard ground, Cain crushing his brother's windpipe in the process. Before Abel had a chance to recover, Cain shoved handfuls of dirt into his brother's eyes and mouth, then he raised his jackal-head

fist again and again, each time cracking the hard weath-
ered ridges of his knuckles against the other man's face.
Crack, crack, crack, crack . . . Until his brother's shouts
stopped and all that was left was the sound of living bone
on dead flesh.

And now he's standing here, staring down at the rem-
nants of his own flesh and blood, the face strangely out
of shape and unrecognisable. What's he done? Where
did it all come from? What was that rush of corrosive
energy all about? Come back, Abel – I feel better now.
Wake up. Wake up, it's okay. You've helped me. I didn't
mean it. Let's go and split a coconut and watch a big-
screen sunset together . . .

Other footsteps crunch in the distance behind him. He
swings round, clenching his bruised knuckles. The figure's still a way off, but he knows who it is. The Boss is
coming. It's Cain's turn to hide now, Cain's turn to relive
that story his mother's often told him, about the day
they hid in the garden and heard the voice of God calling for them. The voice is back, but it's his name on the
breeze now. Hide, Cain, hide, and get used to it: this is
the first day of the rest of your life.

I'm back on the road again, driving, driving, driving.
My head protruding from my neck and nose pressed
to the windscreen in an attempt to see my way through
the horizontal rain that's stabbing repeatedly at my
ailing car, I look for all the world like some street-kid
gazing through the window of the Ritz. Soon I'll call
my wife and tell her what I'm doing. Soon. But not yet.
I'll just enjoy the anonymity of it all for a little longer.
Somehow, as long as no one knows where I am, I feel I
can be anybody and nobody. Rootless and restless.
Like all the great heroes: James Bond, Harry Potter,
Batman, Mr Bean. They're all orphans – all cut loose

from life so they can fight crime and be lonely and miserable.

The towns fly by and I wonder where this pseudo orphan will end up – or at least spend the night. If all goes according to plan, I'll end up at two in the morning still driving round trying to find a travel tavern. And when that doesn't work, I'll drive all the way back home with a slow puncture and indigestion. Indiana Jones never went limping back to his father with his whip between his legs. Why can't I be a super-hero? At least for the weekend.

I talk to myself about this for a while, hoping that God's listening in too. The rain begins to ease. I start to feel better, then I switch on the stereo and catch the first strains of a CD of nursery rhymes. My heart sinks and soars at the same time – which in reality would of course rupture it badly and make a terrible bloody mess in my rib cage. It soars because for three days I don't have to listen to these happy songs of carnage; the religiously persecuted old man hurled down the stairs for not praying, weird little Georgie snogging the girls and scared of the boys, battered Jack lying in a coma at the bottom of his famous hill, his head caved in and seeping blood as Jill lands on top of him and adds injury to injury. Such sweet tales. Macabre stories of death and torment that we've turned into kids' adventures. Just like the Bible then. But my heart sinks too because my head suddenly turns into a picture book, my three kids frolic madly alongside the likes of Pat, Sam, Percy and Bob across my internal big screen – plastic-faced builders, firemen, park keepers and postmen save the world while my starry-eyed tribe look on and wonder.

I push myself back in my seat and put on one of those retro CDs. Elvis Costello, Joe Strummer and Ian Drury spit out their happy tunes – they're not as violent as the kids' ones but they do their best. I sing at the top of my voice and people overtake me and give me strange looks, I wave back as if they're my best friends. They quickly look away. I sing on, louder than ever. I'm flying now – I could drive all night. Nothing's gonna stop me now.

Where do those sudden lapses in energy come from? Do they hide behind hedges and leap out like modernday Dick Turpins, ambushing your senses and making off with your vavavoom? How come one minute I'm the sharpest tool in Do It All – the next I'm a sagging bloodhound, my eyes flickering like a faulty TV, my head lolling about like a cuckoo from a broken clock? Wake up! Concentrate. Turn the music up. Oh, it is up. Stare at that artistic daub of bird excrement on the windscreen, no, don't do that, it's making it worse. Do something difficult. What's 375,968 divided by 21.357? No idea. Who cares? I just want to sleep. No, you don't. How many letters did St Paul write? Don't think about St Paul, he definitely have you in the land of nod. 'Anything in the post today, love?' 'A couple of mortgage offers, a postcard from Peter, oh, and another really long one from St Paul.'

What about Cain? Cain? Yea, why did he kill Abel? That's a good one, that'll keep me from . . . zzzzzz

It's no good. I give in. I pull up in some anonymous town by some anonymous park (I was asleep when I passed the Welcome to Nowhere sign) and lay my head back. I'll just catch forty winks. Sleep won't come, of course, because (a) I'm not driving and in danger of crashing and (b) headrests in cars are designed to be about as comfortable as an electric fire in your underpants. Besides, I'm distracted by Cain now. Why did he kill Abel?

Murder doesn't usually come out of nowhere. You're not walking along, giving a little whistle, when suddenly you decide to annihilate your nearest and dearest. These things grow, they fester, they develop. They have history.

I pick up my little black book and venture into the nearby park. There's something keenly familiar about this place but right now my head's in other places. It's eleven forty-five and a few mums are out with their toddlers, playing on the swings. I spy a graffitied park bench and sit on the spot where *Mags done it with Zed.*

Why did it all go so wrong so quickly? The good book tells me God accepted Abel's offering and rejected Cain's. How did they know? Did fire fall from heaven in true Elijah style or did they go and visit God? Get the Yo and the No face to face. Seems a daft, even heretical notion now, but maybe that's only 'cos we live in an age where God seems more diffident, more cautious. Perhaps in those early days he lived in a Des Res on the prairie and anyone could go and visit him any time. I say anyone, but obviously the neighbourhood wasn't exactly crowded out at that point. If God made people, and if being alone is not good, then surely he wanted to spend lots of time with the ones he'd made. Even after the Eden crash. Even after the infection of sin came via the mouth of one devious parrot snake.

Maybe the Maker spent decades, centuries, on earth interacting with the Adams family. Maybe he went on making people, set up a factory producing body parts and air-blasting them into being. For at least the first 235 years of life no one *worshipped* God. Why? Maybe up to that time they didn't need to, they related to him face to face. Could have been that way for much longer: my fount of knowledge tells me it was during Seth's lifetime that worship leaders first plugged in their harps and sound-checked their lyres, but Seth's lifetime wasn't the usual 65 and retire, 85 and expire. No. He lived on till a whopping 805! What kind of pension was he drawing by the end? And it means it could have been a millennium before God excused himself from chez earth. Maybe it was the flood that brought an end to that particular era.

It still doesn't cast light on killer Cain. Was it just jealousy? Why does anybody kill someone? Anger, revenge, vendetta . . . Most murderers kill people they know. But they do it because of a back story; they have motive, means and opportunity. My guess is Cain's killing instinct had been nurturing for a while, growing in the dark of his soul. It may have been a sudden crime of passion, but what was he passionate about? Maybe like so many of us, or at least like me, he feared and envied someone in his life who had more confidence, more ability, more luck than he did. Or maybe Abel just chewed his food in an irritating, mouth-ever-open, lip-clacking, death-deserving kind of way. (If that's the criteria, then I have a list for killing as long as a Chinese menu.)

Whatever the reason, Cain became a marked man. He and God have a chat and God pronounces sentence on Cain. Cain and God have a few chats in the course of history – before he ever does the dark deed, God warns him of the dark wolf of sin that's lurking, waiting to tear bits out of him. Later Cain complains that his sentence doesn't fit the crime; it's too hard, he says.

And God continues to listen and talk. He makes a promise of protection, and aha! another clue – Cain complains that he has been *banished from God's presence*! Does that not point to God's holiday home being on that bit of planet earth? Either way, Cain packs his bags and moves out and heads for the land of Nod. Apparently this has nothing to do with climbing the wooden ladder but has everything to do with being a perpetual wanderer. A sort of first-century Mad Max.

And later, despite being marked as a man who'll never settle, Cain tries to build a city. He just won't obey the rules. He has *naughty boy* running through his core like Blackpool in a stick of rock. Maybe when Adam and Eve were doing home schooling, he was always the bad boy of the class – even though there were only two lads in there. He probably has a disruptive gene.

Whatever the cause, he won't live a peaceful life. He's a damaged man, hurting, wounded, spilling out bile into the river of life. Was he forever haunted by that day in the field? Did he continue to know God? Or was his worst fear forever realised, kicked out into the unknown, no more chats with his Maker, wandering aimlessly miles from the land of the living?

7. A Few Good Men

Matthew 4:18–22

Where d'you go to find a reliable bunch of mates? Down the pub? In the church? At the football ground?

Jesus starts at the synagogue. He stands there for a while, part of the proceedings, a man hidden by time and tradition. He listens, he looks. But he can't find them. He can't see the spark, the energy, the derring-do, the desire to change. It's just not there amongst the religious. He sighs and strolls home. The old men sit around spitting and swapping stories, soldiers fly by on horses, children play in the streets. No one notices, no one sees the God with flesh on, the man with divinity in his veins. They're too caught up with life to notice Life. He moves on, tries the brothels and the banquets. Men satisfy their sex drive with little thought for their souls; they drink and dine and dance, and often he joins in, but he finds no kindred spirit. He feels at home but not at peace. He wanders down to the Roman garrison. One day these bones will live. These men of steel, these infidels will find a refuge in his Father's house. But not now, now it's all regulations and prostitutes. Something nudges him towards the sea, towards the lake of Galilee. He walks up and down the shore. The place is full of broken boats and cussing, sweating men.

He sees Andrew, Simon, James and John, men he knows will make bad disciples. Too impetuous, too wild, too competitive. They're always taunting one another, always restless to bring in the next catch, always trying to bellow louder than each other.

'They'll do.'

It's a simple two-word phrase and it sneaks into his head and slaps him round the brain.

'You're kidding.'

'Wait and see.'

'But these guys . . . they're so disorganised, so unruly. They wouldn't know discipline if it slapped them round the head and made them stand up straight.'

'Wait and see.'

Jesus walks along the shore. They watch him and he watches them. They're fixing their nets and giving him the evil eye. They've heard about him, one of them bumped into him when the hairy baptist was kicking up a storm. One of these guys was there the day Jesus got baptised, the day thunder rattled in the skies.

'Catch much?' he asks.

They nod and grunt.

'You're pretty good at what you do.'

They nod and grunt again, but now they're wondering – how does he know? Has he been watching them?

Jesus picks up a discarded fish head and feels the weight of it in his hand. His palm is cracked and scarred. He knows what it is to sweat for a living.

'Listen guys, I won't mess about. I've got a good job for you.'

'We already have a job.'

'Sure. But I have a better one.'

The younger one, Andrew, is intrigued. He knows Jesus. John was a good friend of his and John was this guy's cousin.

'I'm looking for followers – guys I can teach. Are you interested?'

Andrew turns to his brother, eyes narrow, 'I told you,' he said. 'I told you he'd come looking.'

'This is the one you told me about? This is . . . him? I thought he'd be taller. I thought you said he was a giant?'

Jesus laughs and kicks at a pile of rotting fish.

'I think you're confusing me with Goliath,' he says. Then he asks them again, 'Are you interested?'

Andrew is, Simon's not so sure. Andrew's used to following, he's Simon's little brother, and he hung out with the weird beard for a while. Juggernaut John.

But Simon's not a follower, he's a leader. Guys always look to him. Even when he's wrong. Why should he bow down to the latest passing rabbi?

'I can make something of you. You can get out of this place.'

Simon looks at Andrew. Only this morning, they've been talking about making it big. The two guys down the lake are putting the pressure on. Their business is booming and they're doing a whole lot better than Si and Andy right now. Simon has no idea why. Lately work has become a treadmill, he doesn't enjoy any of it, everything feels mundane, one day's the same as the next. It wasn't like this before. And it isn't that long ago that they started, it's all become so dull so quickly. Back then it was a massive adventure, the challenge of the dark nights, the voyages into the unknown, the hazardous journeys, the threat of catastrophic storms. It all thrilled him then, set his nerves on edge, made him grit his teeth and ball his fists, pumped the adrenaline deep into his core.

Now every day's the same and lately he's wondered about looking elsewhere for the danger and the darkness.

'Are you interested?'

The man's starting to walk away, he won't wait forever. Andrew makes up his mind and gets busy
bundling his nets back into the boat. But that's Andy –
always does make up his mind quickly, Si thought he'd
lost him when he threw in his oars and went racing after
Big Bad John. But he came back not long after. Now it
looks like he's off again. Simon wipes a hand across his
mouth. He can smell the fish, he has entrails under his
fingernails.

'There's got to be something better,' he mutters to
himself.

'What?'

Andy turns and looks back at him. In the distance,
over his brother's shoulder, Simon spies two Roman soldiers beating the living daylights out of two teenage
kids. Simon can't hear the sound of the violence but he's
heard it many times before. A little child crouches in the
gutter and watches in stunned silence. She's no more
than a tiny speck in Simon's eye. The grinning soldiers
have no regard for her or the trauma they're inflicting.

'There's got to be more than this,' he says. 'Life can't
be this bad.'

'What are you going on about?'

'Nothing.'

Only yesterday he sat on the side of the boat and
watched a fish writhe, flip and pucker in one of the nets,
the life not yet gone from its body, wrestling for a few
more moments of futile existence before it was all too
late. And it forced him to wonder about himself, and his
own writhing and wrestling and existence. He wasn't
one given to reflection or meditation, but for a moment
there he saw a glimpse of the truth and it thoroughly
depressed him.

So now he hurls the heavy nets into the boat and
walks away. He's decided – he'll take a risk. For once

he'll be a follower, as tough as that might prove to be. He has to run to catch up. Jesus is already a good distance down the shore, approaching two other men, and they look for all the world like the two guys who've been out-performing Simon and Andrew lately.

It's lunchtime but I'm not hungry. Why would I be? I've been eating all morning. The mums and their toddlers eventually wander off and that's when the first school kids start to appear. The place quickly fills with the sound of teenage taunting and the ripping of snack packets. That's when I start to feel a certain déjà vu. There's something oddly familiar about this place.

I guess if I'm honest, one reason I'm running away for a while is because my life feels drab. I used to think Christianity would make my life more exciting, but it hasn't turned out that way. Not at all. The narrow road sometimes seems fraught with normality, rainy days and insomnia.

I gaze around this park and everyone else looks as if they have more interesting lives than me, even the stray dogs and the bolshy kids. Okay, so most of them are insecure teenagers and probably come from splintered families but it still feels that way. I look at them now and they seem to have so much going for them that's already up and gone for me. Potential, romance, adventure, danger, the unknown. I know it's easy to tar them all with the same star-spangled brush but it all looks so possible for them and so impossible for me.

I watch four fifteen-year-olds board a seesaw designed for two three-year-olds. It's incredible the way older kids want to be little again, whereas my four-year-old wants to be big. You can't win, can you? Life's better when you're older, till you actually get older, then it was perfect when you were younger. The present moment is an elusive puff of dry ice. It's a fleeting thing. Stand back, hold your breath and cease running and for one heart-stopping freeze-frame moment you might just get a glimpse of the wonder of it all. But try and grip it and it's gone. And then you'll spend the rest of your life waxing on about that one moment when life meant something and you felt like you'd made it; boring your mates down your local night after night, if you still have any by then.

The day my oldest was born, there was a dry ice moment. I drove back through misty country lanes and encountered a stag. It came snaking over the hedge like a stream of divine smoke, hugged the road for a moment, then glided over the other hedge and was gone. And I was left staring after its memory, stunned by its elegance and sleek mobility. I've never forgotten that moment. It seemed somehow to seal a day of mystical power and merciless pain. Heaven invading earth yet again through the body of a suffering woman. I met a guy once who claims every new birth is a fresh footprint of God on the planet. The Maker's spirit invades another family in a covert operation of stealth and struggle, and for a few brief moments men cry and allow themselves the luxury of weakness, carelessly wrapping their arms around strangers and letting the love of others warm their hearts. Rare precious moments. God's clever like that.

I flip to Matthew's biog and in my mind's eye watch a stranger pass by a lake.

If some bloke I'd never met before suddenly pitched up in this park and asked me to go with him . . . well, you know it sounds weird. And though I used to think that Jesus had something *other* about him (in the TV series *Jesus of Nazareth* Robert Powell portrayed this by choosing never to blink as he played Jesus) now I'm not so sure. I'm more convinced that he would have melted into a crowd, looked like a regular Dougal or Colin, or Methuselah more like. Jesus didn't walk around with some strange aura glowing from his eyebrows. He cut his toenails, he got indigestion and he woke up in the night with cramp burning into his legs.

Recently I went to see *The Queen* – the movie not the Lizmeister herself – and I clearly recall the giggles that ruptured from the audience the moment we first saw her royal majestyness in bed with curlers and a fag. Actually she didn't have the fag sadly, but she still looked very ordinary and small tucked up under that corgi-covered duvet. The Queen sleeps! Shock horror! And so did the One who strolled along the shore of Galilee looking for some mates who would help him change the world.

So here he is, walking along in broad daylight, the One who invented walking and broad daylight in the first place. It's an odd idea, isn't it? What if God unmasked looked more human than the rest of us? What would that mean?

And here's Simon, the one who'll form some kind of rocky start to Christendom, the up and down *Yea but no but yea but no but* man who'll one day die for this cause.

'One day, Simon, someone'll bind your hands and take you where you don't want to go . . .'

Hmm, this has way too many similarities with being a father of wilful children who appear with a dressing-gown belt and the intention of making you the subject of their latest kidnapping game. But with Surly Simon, it was all gonna be far more sinister. Soldiers he'd feared when Jesus got the chop would later come looking for him with a cross and three nails – and this time he wouldn't deny anything. Instead, he'd request they make the whole experience worse than ever. What was it Jesus said? 'You'll have what you need when you need it.' Or words to that effect.

'Don't try and work out now whether you've got courage – you'll get it on a need to know basis.'

A friend of mine once described a massive youth gathering where the kids were asked to declare whether they were willing to give up their life for their faith. How could they know that? Jesus himself only found the courage he needed at the moment he needed it.

With hindsight, I can promise you on a blood oath that I would have left my nets and followed the King of Kings. But Simon and Andrew didn't have hindsight. And the King of Kings wasn't wearing a crown. They just had their intuition, the word of a wild man who looked weird, and the invitation of a guy who took an interest in their lives.

So I sit here looking round this park now and I wonder. Would any of us recognise the Maker of all things if he strolled by? Especially if he were just as trendy as the rest of us, didn't have blue eyes and refused to float above the ground. Maybe he's here already. Maybe he's that cocky kid with the shades, spitting in the sandpit and challenging his mate to shin up one of the poles supporting the swings. Maybe he's the old man fumbling with his roll-up, his eyes dull and weeping a little, or maybe he's the guy with the thick tattooed neck and the listless Rottweiler. Or the suited office clerk sitting on the grass poring over his copy of *The Da Vinci Code*, knees pulled up to his chest and back pressed hard against the park railings. (You're never more than six feet away from Dan Brown, you know.) Maybe he's the frightened lad with the glasses lurking by the roundabout and looking for a friend. Maybe he's in all of them. If the day of Pentecost is anything to go by, then God's dished out his hands and feet to the likes of you and me. Not a good idea, God, not a good idea at all. What's plan B? What d'you mean there is no plan B? But plan A is way too precarious. Still no plan B? The words 'eggs' and 'one basket' come to mind. But I digress . . . Basically I can be Jesus to any of these park people, and if I give a smile or a can of Coke to any of them, they can be the Man of Nazareth to me.

8. Romance is Dead

Genesis 24

Rebekah is a sight for sore eyes. She has the kind of face that launched a thousand fights. Lads at school fisting it out to be the first to bed her; boys in the locker room bragging about exploits in the dark. In reality they're brick-scared of her, she's too perfect. The local lads are too riddled with insecure notions ever to risk a put-down from her. She has the well-developed confidence to match her body. It's all out there.

Abraham's broken a vow. He's bought land – but only to bury the girl of his dreams. That's surely within the agreement. He'll wander for the rest of his born days but his wife can rest now, she can lay down her perfect head and sleep forever. He's held himself together till now, but as the shrouded form slips from his sight into the cold cave, it sends a crack through his heart and Isaac has to steady him. It's all suddenly too hard, the old man's been through too much. He turns and buries his head in his son's shoulder and sobs so loud they can hear it in the fields around. Mud-spattered workers stop their ploughing and wonder at the sound of a man shrieking like a wounded jackal. Breastfeeding women start and cover the ears of their babies for a moment. A couple of lovers in a derelict shed sit up, wipe their lips and wonder why the sound puts a sudden stranglehold on their lust.

Two weeks later Isaac, weary and lonely and still grieving, comes limping back through the undergrowth with his head full of thoughts about his Maker and his mother. At times of stress like this, his mind always drifts back to that day on the mountain.

'Where's the sacrifice dad, why aren't we carrying it with us? Why are you so quiet? Why are you crying?'

It was a terribly confusing day, and he's never really recovered. It wasn't good seeing his old man so shaken and disturbed. His dad was a rock, he could do anything, he wasn't supposed to stand there blubbing, with his hands trembling, as he lashed Isaac's arms together. He shudders as he sees himself again in his mind's eye, so small and scared and lying draped across that mountain of kindling. There's fire on the horizon now, or is that dust? Yes, it's dust, a line of camels is approaching. Must be his father's servant back at last. He's been away a while; probably out there on some thankless task looking for more carts or better fabrics for the tents. Since his father has no land to invest in, he spends much of his time trying to improve his mobile home.

He stands and stares at the rising column of dust, spiralling upwards like a pillar of cloud. The grey apparition billows out against the bright blue sky, looking for all the world like the face of God, gazing down on him and his loss. Two weeks ago he lost his mother, when dust took her to dust, twenty-four years ago he lost part of his father when the God of heaven tested the old man's spirit, now the face looks down at him and for a moment it seems to smile. Why? Why smile on a day like this? Why smile at me when I have no goodness in my life? Beneath the cloudy face, the camels draw closer. It is his father's servant Jalam. Faithful old Jalam who'd do anything for his faithful old man. Who's that with him? Grief, it's a woman! And not an old one at that. Isaac's heart skips a beat. He catches sight of her face for a moment then the stranger draws a veil across it. Who is she? What's she doing here? Isaac grins to himself. That is good news, he mutters to the sky. The grey cloudy face is melting away now but there's still a smile up there.

Jalam sees Isaac and comes hobbling across the ground towards him. Years of service and days in the saddle have left the old guy lame, but he does his best to hurry with the good news.

'Sir,' he gasps, 'I have brought someone . . .'

'Who is she? Who's that girl?'

'She's your wife, sir. She's Bethuel's daughter.'

'Bethuel?'

'Your father's great-niece. She's very beautiful sir, believe me.'

'You think I'm only interested in a woman's body?'

'Frankly sir, yes. But she is also intelligent, kind and full of initiative. I prayed that God would lead me to someone like that for you and he did just that.'

'How? How did he do that?' Isaac's annoyed that everyone seems to know about this matchmaking except him, including God.

'I prayed that if she were the right person when I asked her for a drink she'd also offer to water my camels. It showed great kindness and generosity for her to do that.'

'Does she have a sense of humour?'

'I've not told her any jokes, sir.'

'Well ask her this one – why did God ask my father to sacrifice me at the age of twelve?'

'What?'

'Why did God ask my father to sacrifice me at the age of twelve?'

There's a footfall near them. The veiled figure approaches and a strange accent speaks.

'Because if you'd have been a teenager, it wouldn't have been a sacrifice.' She bows her head to him, then adds, 'You're famous where I come from.'

There's no smile, of course, because he can't see her lips, but this girl obviously has wit.

'Isaac, this is Rebekah.'

Jalam steps discreetly away and Rebekah moves closer.

'You're a long way from home,' Isaac says.

'So are you.'

'Walk with me. Jalam, do the right thing and come with us. Just stay out of earshot.'

They walk for a while, crossing the fields where the workers and the mothers and the lovers froze at the sound of Abraham's grief. Isaac's heart is in his mouth, his hands won't stop sweating. Rebekah seems very calm indeed.

'I lost my mother,' he says eventually, and for some reason his voice breaks as he says it.

'I know. You loved her a lot.'

'Well, don't you love your mother?' he snaps. 'Sorry. I'm . . . uptight.'

'You have good reason. Everyone's been fixing your future for you, Isaac, including me. I have heard a lot about you, and I've waited a long time for this moment.'

They don't say much more than that. But Isaac knows, he's hooked, he's falling for this girl and he'll marry the first and only love of his life. As the creeping black night gets a grip on the land, he takes her to his tent and they attempt to make love. The experience is awkward and clumsy and not half as good as he thought it was going to be. But lying with her afterwards in the dark makes him feel better about life. He's still in a bad place and the warmth of her body brings him some peace. They lie together for a long time, not really sleeping and eventually, as the light breaks over the camp, they try again. It's still pretty bad and wouldn't make it into *The Good Sex Guide*, but they have plenty of time. If his parents are anything to go by, they have decades to get this love machine in the right gear.

There's a radio playing somewhere, probably from one of the open windows in the nearby terraces. It's tuned to Radio 2 and Steve Wright is frothing at the mouth and playing Golden Oldies. *Midnight Train to Georgia* comes on and I come over all wistful. There's always been something painfully sad about that song – even though it tells a happy story.

I'd rather live in your world than be alone in my own.

So, leave behind what you know, what you love, all that you've built up and gathered round you – abandon it all for what? A precarious future that may well turn out to be as futile as the belief that England will one day again win the World Cup, or that Tim Henman will lift that Wimbledon trophy.

Abe left his world, upped and went looking for a better life, in search of another mountain, another land of promise. Did that dream comfort him on the day he buried his wife on a bit of hastily purchased turf in a foreign field somewhere? Ultimately, of course, Abe died without ever living the dream. He saw a world that would benefit everyone except himself. He didn't suffer from the shortsighted faith I'm stuck with; it seems he could see forever. So many prophecies get bandied around these days, so many promises and pictures but few of them have a long sell-by date. They're about today and tomorrow and maybe a week on Wednesday. Where are the Daniels and the Abrahams and Isaiahs? The ones who'll see beyond themselves and their tiny three score years and ten? The ones who'll dare to dream dreams and see visions for the great, great, great grandkids?

I glance around the park and my eye sees all those things I missed before. Now that I've taken in the big picture I start to notice the small print; that optimistic collection of milk cartons sliced in two and turned into window boxes for a few wilting daffodils. The car with the smashed back window, the little cubes of turquoise glass scattered like a thousand slug pellets across the boot. Does the owner know yet? Or do they still have the *joy* of making that soul-destroying discovery? My selfish instinct kicks in and I glance over in the direction of my own car, thinking only of my own welfare now. There's nothing like a spot of wanton destruction for stealing your faith in humanity. In my head I round up the villains and beat them senseless with a broken fence post. Then I feel guilty, revive them, convert them to the faith and induct them into theological college, where they no doubt spend their days joy-riding in the principal's 4x4. I give up dreaming and stare at the one bright blue house in the terrace of dirty cream buildings that runs parallel to the far end of the park. The discarded damp sock hanging from one window ledge. The faded *Jesus is coming back – look busy!* poster peeling off a boarded doorway. The ornately sprayed slogan beneath the windows bellowing some man-sized message about the wonder of *Mutant Mountain Bikes*. Above the word 'mutant', there's a little old lady peering through the net curtains that have been there since Queen Victoria visited this park and probably told people she was really not amused by the jaunty graffiti and the steaming piles of dog-curd. And here in the park I'm surrounded by irregular circles of rotting apples and discarded Twix wrappers looking for all the world like stagnant pools of wormy murk in a sea of scuffed turf. There's a shocking tinge of horror and apocalypse about it all. I always struggle with normality – it has the power to make me feel very depressed indeed.

Another sad song comes on the distant radio and I instantly feel better. Freddie Mercury's venting his operatic spleen in a number about spreading his little wings and flying away from it all. Just what I'm longing for right now. The song's as bleak as hell and it lifts my spirits no end.

But then music's like that – the most heart shredding of ballads can sound like a fortnight in Disneyland if you're in the right mood. *Baker Street*'s as sad as they come but because I once heard it when I was fourteen – and fully convinced that one day I'd turn out to be James Bond married to every single one of Charlie's Angels – it's a song of wistful hope and undying potential. I still believe life can turn out well when I catch the strains of that saxophone. Shame I can't say the same about so many worship songs. The truth can set you free – even when it's harsh dismal unpleasant truth; whereas some of those happy holy numbers can wax on about freedom for all their worth but still do little more than tie you up in all kinds of platitudinal knots. The right words and the right message don't always go hand in hand.

The inimitable Scott Walker strikes up with his song about first love never dying. I hope you're wrong, Scott, I really do. I mean, that's okay for the likes of Isaac and Rebekah. Two starry-eyed young things, never been in love, never had hearts broken, never argued about putting the loo seat down or plucking the hairs from the bath tub. When your first love is your forever love, that's all well and good. But when your first love becomes your forever *lost* love, you're in trouble. And if that love never dies, then many of us blokes are trapped in the bottomless pit of regret forever.

It's so much easier to fall back in love with that former long-lost girlfriend. The one that got away. She was perfect, she was beautiful, she was flawless and forever young. But then I never tried to marry her, have a honeymoon with her, raise her kids or pay off her phone bill. I never had to go shoe shopping with her, or wash her underwear.

A group of mothers bustle into the park with their pre-school children, released from playgroup for good behaviour. Somehow the time's moved on to three o'clock. I've frittered away three hours on this park bench. I don't mean to stare at the women chin-wagging by the swings, you can get arrested for this kind of thing, but something's stirring in my head.

She looks for all the world like a girl I once dated. A girl I once loved and lost. She's older of course, and no doubt wiser, but I'm sure it's her, she still has that smile, those eyes, and oh, I dunno, everything the love of my life once had. Before I know it, I'm scheming about how to get over there and chat her up. I mean, catch up with her. Talk about the past, about what she's up to now, about our respective partners and how happy we both are these days. And then take her off somewhere for a coffee and (what was it she always loved? Oh yes) lemon meringue pie, while her obliging mates look after her kids for ten hours. Before I know it I'm up and heading over there and with every step the truth becomes clearer. It really is her, after all these years. The girl I often wondered about and, yes, dreamt about and made up all kinds of things about.

She looks at me strangely. I mutter some words about it being me after all this time. Now they're *all* looking at me strangely. I ask her if it's really her, after all this time.

One of her kids comes and stares up at me. His nose is running and there's so much chocolate round his mouth he looks like Ronald McDonald. Her eyes narrow, she's about to walk away, then suddenly she points at me and laughs. Is that a good sign or a bad one? She says my name and laughs again. Why all this laughing?

I don't like all this laughing. Her friends say my name and laugh too. She asks what happened to me. I tell her I moved away. She starts talking about her children and how she'd forgotten all about me, and halfway through that sentence I decide I don't fancy her at all. I turn and start to walk away but she won't let me go, she wants to keep talking.

She wants to tell me about her problems and her house in the poor part of town. She's changed. She's turned into a real woman. And I think she's had a lot of lemon meringue pie. She used to want to talk about my album collection and how good I was at skimming stones. Even though I was very bad at it. I realise now she's much more attractive in my head where she hasn't had to suffer childbirth, years of housework and a succession of bad men. I much prefer her in there. She doesn't try to tell me too much, she just turns up and makes me laugh and lets me do all the talking. In my head she's obsessed with my good looks and my sexual prowess. Now, in this park, she's just obsessed with her lack of money and how many more kids she might have. It turns out she's currently married to a guy who used to scare the hell out of me at school.

The conversation seems to go on forever. Her friends start to look familiar, but they've changed too. They're fatter and thinner and older and noisier and I realise now that I've ended up in a town I once lived in for a fleeting impressionable six months. It sounds daft but I arrived here in such a daze it's taken me this long to recognise where I've landed. I lived here at that glorious time when girls were the new undiscovered country and it was like I'd just got my passport. Now that I think about it, there were quite a few countries I would have liked to visit but never got round to it. We moved house. That's why it all came to nothing. We moved away and

I left the girl I adored. Now I start to wonder if I had a close shave, I mean, I'm sure she's a great person – she's just not my great person. I doubt if I'll visit her again in my head. They're still chatting as I make my excuse and tear myself, apparently reluctantly, away.

It was lucky for Isaac that Rebekah turned out to be all he thought she was from a distance. Not only was she smart and sassy – she turned out to be a great lover too. And three out of three ain't bad – it's very good indeed. Of course, like the long-lost love of my life, she did change with time. She became devious as well as intelligent, scheming as well as smart. And where he favoured the wild boy Esau, she preferred gentle Jacob, the one who inherited her devious, scheming gene.

In the park they're still laughing about me as I climb into my car. I start the engine hastily and stall it. I glance over at them and wave through the green railings. They're still laughing at me. I fire up the engine once more and that's when I notice the parking ticket on the windscreen.

9. Knock, Knock, Knockin' on Heaven's Door

Habakkuk 1:2–4; 3:3–7; 3:17–19

How long, O LORD, must I call for help? I pray, I fast, I shout at the heavens but you just don't listen! It's not fair. Life's unfair. I beat my fists against the black skies until they drip blood all over my twisted rage-wrung face but nothing comes back. I watch the news night after night and all I see is violence. I tell you about it, a million others cry out to you, but you do not come to save us. Children get bought and sold on a daily basis; they are kidnapped and abused. People grow up in misery and oppression and nothing changes. Nothing! Must I forever see this sin and misery all around me? Wherever I look, I see destruction and violence. The newspapers are full of people who love to argue and fight. On and on and on. They revel in stupid disunity and petty conflicts. The law has become paralysed and useless, and there is no justice given in the courts. Lawyers twist and mutilate the law. You love justice but you remain aloof about it. The wicked far outnumber the righteous, and justice is perverted with bribes and trickery. What's going on, Lord? What's going on?

A parking ticket! A parking ticket! How dare they? Here I am – a stranger in a strange land and I get jumped on.

No wonder people hate this country. I throw myself out of the car and rip the ticket from the windscreen, which is not easy cos the glue's pretty strong.

I pace up and down for a while, spitting and hissing at the pavement, waving the plastic-wrapped ticket in my fist as if it's a gecko I'm trying to kill by shaking it by the tail. (This, by the way, would never work as geckos shed their tails as frequently as we sneeze.) I suddenly remember that I have an audience and I risk a glance back at the swings in the park. Thank goodness – the women have left. I don't know when or how, but they aren't here to see me cussing and fuming about a faggin' parking ticket. I take the poisonous packet, walk back through the gates and limp over to my bench. Except it's no longer my bench. *Mags done it with Zed* now has two school kids cavorting all over it. How dare they? Don't they know I've just invested three hours of my life in that seat? This is just like Cutter's. On your worst days, heartless hooded outlaws come out of the shadows and take possession of your cosy armchair by the fire.

The two kids on the bench stop fighting and look at me.

They don't say anything but their faces tell the story.

'Yea, loser? What you looking at?'

I turn away. I'm bored of that bench anyway. I wander across the grass. Four girls stand on the swings sucking on cigarettes and practising swear words. Three thirty. School's out and the place is awash with kids who should be at home hoovering, ironing and doing their homework. Seen and not heard.

I make for a bench on the far side of the park. Oh great, it's broken and there's seagull excrement all over it. Boy, those seagulls really know how to go for it. They must have been out for a vindaloo last night. It's everywhere. I don't want to be seen wiping the seat with a tissue cos all

The Road Trip

the cool school kids will then know what a pettifogging wimp I really am. And then they'll no doubt mug me, smash the rear window of my car and plant drugs on me so I end up doing life. And all because I can't sit on *Mags done it with Zed*. Life is too harsh sometimes. Why is this happening? Traffic wardens are just vicious, nefarious bar stewards. They take pleasure in evil and delight themselves in wickedness. Their hordes advance like a wind from the desert, sweeping captives ahead of them like sand. It's not right. It's not right! I only came here for a rest. I didn't know I was gonna offend her royal majestyness by parking on that extremely faint double yellow line. I was not intent on doing anything lawless.

For a while I consider deliberately fighting this piece of injustice all the way to the Old Bailey. I might have to mortgage my house and sell my children to a well-known but unnameable sports brand for cheap labour but it'll be worth it. *Panorama* will sing my praises and Esther Rantzen will do a teatime special all about me.

Instead I turn to that other piece of media – my little black book, and I flip to Habakkuk. *I will climb up into my watchtower now and wait to see what the LORD will say to me and how he will answer my complaint*. Ah; no watchtower around, so I'll just keep sitting on this bench, but I'll still wait. Hmm, interesting. Hab complains to God – lets out his frustration and anger, vents his righteous spleen and pours out his fear and doubts and what does he get? A vision of God! That's not fair. Hab might have been furious about a painful, writhing planet, but what about me? I'm annoyed about a parking ticket. Where's my vision of God? Hab got brilliant splendour, light, pestilence and shattered mountains. What do I get? Six teenagers, four fags and a broken park bench. Where's the vision of God in this?

I see God, the Holy One, moving across the deserts from Edom and Mount Paran. His brilliant splendour fills the heavens, and the earth is filled with his praise! What a wonderful God he is! Rays of brilliant light flash from his hands. He rejoices in his awesome power. Pestilence marches before him; plague follows close behind. When he stops, the earth shakes. When he looks, the nations tremble. He shatters the everlasting mountains and levels the eternal hills. But his power is not diminished in the least! I see the peoples of Cushan and Midian trembling in terror.

It's interesting to note that when Hab claimed to see God, what he actually saw was God's creation. God's image was seen in his design work. There was no giant face in the sky, no figure appearing beside his tent, no Carpenter walking beside the shore saying 'Follow me.'

I guess if creation is God's calling card, then it must be frustrating when people demand more. Or indeed when they big up the calling card but don't bother to check out who left it behind. If creation gives us an image of God's face, then asking him to show himself is a bit like asking Bob Geldof to do something to help the poor – how much more do we want, for goodness sake? Of course it's our own choice; if we choose to switch on the TV, see an episode of *West Wing* and then swear blind it's the *Teletubbies* – well, that's not the programme makers' fault. If we see creation and swear blind it's mother nature – that's not the creation Maker's fault. He's done all he can. He's left little clues all over the known universe. We want God to do more to reveal himself, crying out 'Show your power,' 'We want to see Jesus,' 'Give us a sign,' and 'Is anyone out there?' We want him to do the work. Sorry, lads, he's already done plenty; what's required now is for us to do some. Ask, seek, knock, dig around, ferret about, have a good old gander – God's done plenty and he won't do more, cos he knows that just dishing out the divine on a plate doesn't make men into his mates. It just makes them fat and greedy. Come on, lads, go on a God hunt, start doing some exercise – flex your mind, your strength, your soul and your will. It's up to you. If you want mother nature you can have her, but seems to me she's a lot smaller and quainter than a Father God. You decide. One thing's for sure about creation, there's plenty of it. As one guy said – it's a small world but you wouldn't want to paint it.

Oh and we're not just talking about the nice things, the butterflies and the rainbows. Hab sees God in the fierce and furious things; in the pestilence and plague, in the quaking hills and erupting mountains. How does he see God in such deadly things? Somehow Hab finds traces of his friend in the forces that at first appear to be anti-God. Maybe all things can somehow show us God's face. Even – my goodness, can it be true? – traffic wardens? And – throttle my neck! – teenagers?

Surely not. Can those smoking, swearing, hooded creatures bear the image of God? I look at them and I know I'm already scowling. I'd not make the best of youth workers. What do I see in those kids? They're energetic. Reckless. Aren't bound by tradition. Most of them think the world needs changing one way or another. A mate of mine who teaches movie studies tells me he can't get his students to critique *The Matrix* – it's just so full of teenage angst they can't be objective about it. It's their take on life. The world is wrong and a covert group of people must change it. Where've I heard that before?

And traffic wardens? Okay, this is a tough one. Where's the imprint of God inside that hat and uniform? I surely don't want to revert back to those days when I saw the Boss as a dictatorial, authoritarian figure, ready to jump on me and slap a ticket across my forehead for the slightest misdemeanour. No way.

But justice matters to the God of heaven. Justice and righteousness should flow like traffic through our streets, instead of the garbage we often see blowing about. And yes, I guess I have to concede that somewhere inside that dark armour there's a human being, somewhere inside that ticket-wielding tyrant there beats a God-made human heart. And wherever there's a human heart – there's the great Architect who designed it.

I flip to the end of Hab's trilogy and find the biggest whammy of all. It's clear that there will be times of hunger and loss, death and destruction. But they don't tell us that God is extinct. Any more than the good times tell us God is alive. This world tells the story – it's here to announce God's presence. Creation continues week in, week out reminding us that his presence is with us. He lives on through the good and the bad. Lurking in the concrete and the clay, in the heroes and villains. His existence is not dependent on Happy Mondays and Lazy Sundays.

Yea, dare I say it – even though I get a parking ticket and lose my place on a park bench, even though I'm intimidated by the locals and annoyed by the seagulls, even though I walk through the valleys of depression and doubt – yet I will be joyful in the God of my salvation.

> Even though the fig trees have no blossom, and there are no grapes on the vine; even though the olive crop fails, and the fields lie empty and barren; even though the flocks die in the fields, and the cattle barns are empty, yet I will rejoice in the LORD! Though the days seem hard and long, though the nights bring loneliness and empty

despair. Though my dreams turned to dust and life did not turn out the way I expected . . . I will still rejoice in the LORD, I will be joyful in the God of my salvation. The Sovereign LORD is my strength! He will make me as sure-footed as a deer and bring me safely over the mountains. He will bring me through the ordeals of unemployment and family breakdown. Though life is tough as a granite boulder, I will do my best to remember him and celebrate his presence; rejoicing in him with frustration in my eyes and disappointment in my heart. I will give him honour and trust that he will give me the strength to see this life through.

10. Stark Buttock Naked

Isaiah 6:1–10; 20:1–6

King Uzziah's dead. After fifty-two years this warrior king is no more. In his heyday he commanded a vast army, employed thousands of leaders and commissioned brilliant technicians to design fighting machines to protect the walls of Jerusalem. This king had been big. And he knew it. That's probably why he was struck with leprosy. Success like that can go to your head, make you irresponsible, stubborn, stupid. Stories about him are rife. It's said that power corrupted him. It invaded his little grey cells and made him believe he could approach God without the use of the appointed priests. When he waltzed into the Temple and started waving incense around, an army of holy men broke in and demanded he give it up immediately. He wouldn't. And thus began the story of the skin disease. It's said that even as he railed against the priests, the skin on his forehead began to crack and rot and peel off like old wallpaper, and the next thing you know, the great king is falling to bits. Literally. Finger by finger. Until this day: the day he died. The *Judean Times* obituary section may big him up as a visionary, a hero, a skilled leader – but one thing's for sure, he wasn't immortal – he's gone.

And the day he died was the day I saw the Lord. Servants were rushing around the Temple corridors like

The Road Trip

dead leaves blustering in a gale, kicked back and forth by the events of the day. I sat at my desk and scribbled it all down. Then for no reason my eyes blurred over. I thought I was tired, or ill, but then my vision cleared and I found myself in the Temple. I was terrified then because that's where the king had contracted leprosy. I'm not a priest and I wanted out of there as soon as possible. But I couldn't move. I was rooted to the spot. And that's when I saw him. He was sitting above me, raised up on a gemstone throne surrounded by an emerald rainbow. A crack of thunder shook me to the core and lightning flashed and flicked from the throne like jagged spears of burning gold.

In front of the throne there was a glistening sea that shone like crystal. And hovering around him were mighty seraphim, living beings, each with six wings. A lion, an eagle, an ox and a man: they used four of their wings to cover their faces and their feet, and with the remaining two they flew. Around and around, the wings beating like the blades of a helicopter. These giant angels sang and their thunderous voices shook the Temple to its foundations, the thunder and lightning cracked and flashed around the building and the entire sanctuary was filled with smoke.

Then I said, 'So this is it. My destruction is sealed, for I am a sinful man and I was born and raised with sinful people. I can't look on the LORD Almighty and live! This is my punishment!' And I said 'Please don't kill me, Lord. I do the same sins week in week out, I'm not a good person, I wilfully do wrong. I can't be here in your presence like this – I deserve to die. I know what I should do but I don't do it. I can't control my mind; it races away before I can stop it. I can't keep a lid on my eyes, they're always off feasting on the things that'll destroy me. And my tongue's no better, it's like a wounded animal, flailing about, spitting out this and that. I tell other people all the good things to do but I can't do them myself.'

My words trailed away and emptiness hung in the air.

Then one of the seraphim flew over to the altar and picked up a burning coal with a pair of tongs. The coal blazed like the mouth of a volcano and as he flew, the rushing air fanned the fire so much that I could see the thing throbbing. He flew back to me, came to rest gently beside me and touched my lips with the blazing crimson fossil. I recoiled, feeling the heat as he drew closer, and I expected searing pain to eat into my face, but I felt nothing. A voice said, 'You're okay, this coal has touched your lips. It cleanses you. Your guilt is gone, it's been taken away and your sins are forgiven.'

Then I heard the Lord ask a question. 'I need a messenger. Whom should I send to speak to my people? Who will dare go for us?'

I leapt forward and said, 'Me! Lord, I'll go! Pick me! Send me!'

And he said, 'Yes, you can go. But tell my people this: "You will hear my words, but you will not understand. You will see what I do, but you will not perceive its meaning." Harden the hearts of these people. Close their ears, and shut their eyes. That way, they will not see with their eyes, hear with their ears, understand with their hearts, and they will not turn to me for healing.'

I recoiled and said, 'Sorry? You want me to do what? Deliver a vital message so that they can ignore it?'

You've got the picture Isaiah, you'll make a great prophet.

Three years later and here he is stark buttock naked, walking around like a piece of raw pork. This isn't what he had in mind when he stood in that Temple and saw that holy place and volunteered. Surely this can't be spiritual. Back then, in that majestic shining place, he was covered in glory, now he's covered in goosebumps. Back then, he felt called; now he just feels cold. People walk by and make jokes about how well endowed he isn't. Children giggle and point, teenage girls throw him their underwear, old women talk about him behind his backside. They call him mad and an exhibitionist – and the worst of it is, he agrees. When God asked him to reveal the truth, this isn't quite the exposure he had in mind.

He skulks into a cave to escape for a while. He buries his face in his hands and sobs tears of embarrassment and frustration.

'Lord, I can't do this,' he mutters, his voice a congealed mess of tears, spit and anger. 'They think I'm an idiot, they think I'm a fool, I'm supposed to be a prophet but they give me no dignity or respect. I'm completely humiliated by my own people's behaviour. Completely humiliated.'

He spits out these last words and they're edged with a dark, bitter regret. What's the point? What is the point?

Then somewhere in his head he hears a familiar voice, a voice once shrouded in smoke and glory, a voice now tinged with the same tone of disappointment and regret.

'Welcome to my world.'

Just four words. If nothing else good comes from this, at least he's discovering how his God feels.

The afternoon sun breaks through for the first time and I feel that welcome blast of warm air on my face. The clouds fight back and for a while the sun battles for supremacy, flashing rhythmically like God blinking at me from his front window. The kids melt away to their X-boxes and pizzas and a few dog walkers emerge. Mongrels rub shoulders with Alsatians and labradors, the gruff and the great and the good sniff each other's rear ends while their owners banter about their life since this time yesterday. A right old mishmash of hats they're wearing too. Baseball caps, woolly numbers, flat caps, a turban . . . one guy even sports a pork pie hat. And then there's the scarecrow skinhead walking his mastiff all alone by the railings. He doesn't wear a hat, just a patch-work of scars. I watch them all and find myself wonder-ing about their lives and their eating habits, their secrets and lovers, what TV they watch, and their take on God. A couple of them look straight at me and I stare back, startled for a moment, and suddenly find a nearby patch of grass very interesting indeed. I need an escape hatch.

Quick – look at someone who can't look back. An Old Testament prophet, he'll do, the Christmas kid who swapped his clothes for a place in history. I find myself staring at this magnificent passage from Isaiah – it's one of the most quoted texts in Christendom. It's a particu-larly useful verse when looking for volunteers to do the tea rota or the flowers. Or – gulp, cough and swallow hard – street evangelism. 'Who will go for us?' goes out the hopeful cry, usually from the vicar or his sidekick. Fifty pairs of eyes look at fifty pairs of shoes. There's a shuffling of papers as the man up front fumbles through his Bible, looking for something with which to prod the congregation, then there's a clearing of the throat and you know it's gonna be that passage from Isaiah. He's hoping for a unanimous cry of: 'Here I am, send me!' And suddenly, unlike Isaiah after his lip-smacking, sin-quenching hot-coke experience, we feel full of guilt and badness. The preacher megaphones Isaiah's gleeful response at us as if it's the most natural thing in the world. Who will go for God? Well, us, of course, look no further, we thought you'd never ask! It's the question we've all been waiting for. A dull, never-ending job? A thankless task? An embarrassing problem? Oh yes please. Sir! Sir! Pick me! Pick me! Pick me!

When what we're really thinking is, er me? No, that can't be right. You're confusing me with someone who cares. You're mixing me up with some who gives a shilling. You've taken me for someone who wants to change the world. Who will go for us? Er . . . Well . . . what about that guy who's not here this week? Put his name down. Or perhaps . . . old whatsisface? Ooh, try them over there. They look keen. They're new. I'll just keep quiet; someone else'll stick their hand up.

Did that happen to Isaiah? Did everyone else take a step back when they were asking for volunteers? So then he had to appear keen to look good, save face, even though his mouth was dry and he was scared spitless.

'Hang on, where'd all the others go? Is it just me, then? Er, can I just make a few calls, Lord? Phone a friend, ask the audience? Oh, there is no audience, and my friends have scarpered.'

Of course, there were no others, unless a lot of other prophets were having the same vision that day and the Temple was crowded with Amos, Hosea, Micah, Nahum, Jonah and Derek from the non-conformist church.

Perhaps if the jobs we were offered were a little more challenging, a little more rough round the edges. After all, Isaiah wasn't being offered crèche duty. At the back of my little black book I've got a newspaper cutting wedged between the cover and the book of Annihilation, sorry Revelation, it's not from any paper I ever saw, and it's nothing like any ad you'll read today.

Men wanted for hazardous journey. Small wages. Bitter cold. Long months of complete darkness. Constant danger. Safe return doubtful. Honour and recognition in case of success. An Arctic explorer by the name of Ernie Shackleton placed it way back in the dark days of 1913. Not quite the same as a plea for flower arrangers or tea pourers.

The response wasn't the same either. Five thousand men applied for twenty-six places.

Perhaps we need a similar approach.

People needed for dangerous after-service challenge, involving contact with evil-tasting coffee and constant danger of green cup handles coming loose. Extreme exposure to industrial strength caffeine and precarious mountains of chipped saucers. Might get a few more hands up? Certainly Isaiah was up for a tough job when he saw one, as scared as he was in the presence of True Greatness. I sit on this bench and my eyes flick back and forward over letters and words that try their best to tell me a story too big for the printed page, too massive for my tiny mind.

It's a also passage full of contradictions. First thing to note here is that Isaiah *saw the Lord*! Hang on; back up there a minute. He saw the Lord? I mean, he really saw the Lord? Not just like Job and Hab who got their glimpses of God from the raging planet? Nope. He saw the Real Deal. And awesome he was too. He was . . . Oh! Isaiah doesn't describe him. He tells impressive tales of six-winged creatures and a smoke-filled sanctuary but there's no description of the Big Man. Why not? This is our big chance to find out if God really does resemble Father Christmas or Morgan Freeman. But no. There's nothing. No identikit picture. Was he beyond words? Too big to lay down in small print? Too frightening? They'd been told not to make any images – was drawing a picture too much like building a golden calf? Then Isaiah gets scared stiff that he's going to die because of his good fortune but one of the seraphim singes his lips and everything's hunky dory. And finally he's told to go and speak to the people, but having volunteered for the job, he's told the best news of all. No one'll listen, mate. He'll be preaching to the hard of hearing – not unlike most Sunday mornings these days. In fact he's ordered to make the people *not* listen. Go and speak the word and make sure no one takes a blind bit of notice! Once again, not unlike most Sunday mornings. He's not the first guy to volunteer to do a thankless task for God. 'Noah, build a boat big enough for a lot of people who'll never get on it.'

I glance up at the dog walkers. Thankfully they're ignoring me now: maybe that makes me a potential prophet. Would they listen to a prophet? Would they scoop up their chihuahuas and their Rottweilers and bundle them aboard a big boat? Would religious words cut any ice with them anyway? A generation who went to church when there were still choristers and lots of people in the pews?

Isaiah turned out to be quite an upbeat kind of guy. His book's full of hopeful poetry, people walking in darkness and seeing the light, bent reeds not broken off, young men running and taking off on eagles' wings and all that. But it wasn't all beer and skittles, he also got the toughest job in prophetville.

'Isaiah?'

'Yes, Lord.'

'I have another task for you.'

'Fantastic. I'll do anything Lord. Lead worship in the band, go to college and become a priest, tell stories in the street and lie prostrate in the Temple.'

'No, much more holy than that. Take your kit off, Isaiah, and walk around stark buttock naked for three years.'

Oh, great. Elijah did some weird things to jam a spanner in the works but this tops them all. Micah and Saul had a dabble in naturism; Micah even did animal impressions at the same time – but not for 1,095 days! Apparently the Assyrians were about to come over the horizon, round up the mighty Egyptians and run off with all their clothes. Isaiah was demonstrating the fate that can befall the big and bad. The harder they come, the harder they fall. Why don't more Christians walk around in the nude today? It might get folks' attention. We love to talk about prophets and seers, well, it seems to me the biblical prophets did all they could to stop people in their tracks. Micah wailed and howled, bringing all the jackals and ostriches around to his door. Ezekiel knocked a hole in his wall and did the kind of DIY that nowadays would get him his own programme on ITV . . .

When ordinary radical Shane Claiborne was introduced in a school gathering as the coolest Christian ever, he asked for a pair of scissors and in front of the school cut off his funky dreadlocks. 'Christians are not called to be cool,' he told them, 'we are called to be extraordinary.' That's why he and a lot of his friends took $20,000 to Wall Street and scattered it all over the place in one giant jubilee demonstration.

Now that's what I call being prophetic.

Sadly I'm not an activist. I'm a passivist. I don't like commitment, I don't want to take responsibility and decide for myself. I want God to do it all for me. One of the main reasons I don't like choice is that I fear making the wrong one. I fear I'll take a step in the wrong direction and God will come down heavily on me – in spite of the overwhelming evidence to the contrary. Think of old wrinkly Methuselah – why'd he live so long? Because according to his name, his death would bring judgment. And God never wants to judge us.

Could I have done an Isaiah? I doubt it. Even if I had just been sidewhacked by a vision of the God of heaven, I'm just too scared a person. Oh, I'm good at bluffing it out, at waffling about vision and destiny and changing the planet – but on the inside I'm just a quivering pile of pigswill.

And even if, in a sudden spurt of divinely-inspired courage, I did put my hand up to the *who will go* question, I fear that a couple of days later I'd be creeping out the back door trying to find a boat to Tarshish.

So I pick up my black book and my parking ticket and head off into the late September sunlight. Who will go for us? Well, right now, me. But not to change the world. If I'm where I think I am, then I'm on my way to see an old friend. A guy who lives not a million miles from here, right out in the middle of nowhere. Just a half hour drive and I'll be there, away from all this real life.

11. An Old Man with a Big Stick

Luke 18:1–8

It's official – God is an old man with a big stick. He sits up in the sky somewhere, rocking raggedly back and forth with a dirty old rug on his knees, shouting at people and whacking them over the head with his big stick.

You can come to him with your twisted, wasted lives and he won't take a blind bit of notice. He's unfair, unjust, bad-mouthed and angry.

Well, he is if you believe Jesus' parable.

'You see,' says Jesus, settling down on a craggy rock, 'there used to be a judge in the city near here. An atheist with a heart as black as charred wood. His family disowned him, his wife and kids gave up on him, he lived alone in a penthouse flat that he never cleaned. The place stank to high heaven, and was infested with rats and cockroaches, although the rats did their best to consume the cockroaches. The place was a hell-hole but it didn't matter because no one ever came near there anyway. The judge had no friends and got no visitors. Until this day, the day when this old, old woman comes, her back bent and her feet malformed and swollen. There's a sharp rap at the door and when the judge answers it – there she is, wanting a bit of justice.

'I don't do justice. Go away.'

But she wasn't listening, she was pouring out her nagging heart.

'Old woman – get lost. You're wasting my time.'

More insistent chivvying from her outdoors.

'Bye then.'

And he shuts the door and leaves her whining on the doorstep. But she's so loud that the people below can hear her and before long they're banging on the ceiling and ringing on the phone.

'What's that appalling racket?'

'It's an old girl with a speech impediment.'

'A speech impediment?'

'Yea, she can't stop.'

'Well, shut her up or we'll get the law round.'

'I am the law!'

'Yea right, and I'm Nelson Mandela. You wouldn't know the law if it set fire to your underpants. Shut her up.'

But he couldn't. He opened the door and she was louder than ever. The more he tried to suppress her, the more insistent she became. In the end, he picked her up and bundled her into his cupboard. He kept her locked up for three weeks feeding her unbuttered, thin sliced white toast under the door, but she just wouldn't switch off. The rats and the cockroaches couldn't stand it and moved out. He got no sleep and couldn't hear the television when it was on. In the end he decided to take radical action. There was just nothing else for it.

'All right, you stupid woman!' he yelled, bundling her out of the cupboard. 'I'll help you! What do you want? Just shut up.'

Jesus looked around at the sea of quizzical frowns.

'So you see – the unjust judge came through in the end. No matter how unjust he seemed, the woman got justice. How about you? Do you have that kind of faith?

Are you prepared to fight and badger and wrestle for
what's right?'

My mate has an old cottage on a bit of land in the middle of nowhere. Four acres of peace and quiet and
anonymous seclusion. That'll do me just fine for the next
forty-eight hours. It's close by now too, just a cough and
a splutter and I'll be there.

If it weren't for this traffic jam.

Ah, traffic jams – that strange impotent place where
the other side of men leaks out.

Where did all these cars suddenly emerge from?
Haven't you got anything better to do than clog up the
roads for those of us running away from ourselves? Go
home. Go home for Gromit's sake! Don't you know
you're destroying the environment? Even as I speak your
4x4 is melting another bit of the ozone. Hurry up! I have
a date with nowhere! Get out of my way! I feel the anger
and resentment building in me like a mega-tsunami.
Soon it will spill out of my gut and spatter the atmosphere with a tidal wave of ranting and random abuse.
Ahh, there's nothing like driving for bringing out your
spiritual side. I once got embroiled in a minor road rage
incident when I gave *the finger* to a driver behind who
blasted me for being indecisive. He proceeded to follow
me, then accosted me at traffic lights, scaring the heebie-
jeebies out of me with the following chilling one-liner:

'You should be careful, you don't know who I am.'

I punched his lights out, obviously.

Maybe if he were around today Jesus would have
said, 'Where your car is, that's where your heart will be.'

Of course, having said that, I do know he is around
today. Honest. But now I feel doubly bad: I'm stuck in
traffic losing precious time and I just intimated that
Jesus is not here with me. Is he with me? Of course. In

spite of the claim that guardian angels leave your car when you go over the speed limit – I don't think Jesus does. I think he likes a challenge.

But is he happy? I throw a glance over to my passenger seat, almost expecting to see him there, armed with a bucket of plagues and a baseball bat. Instead I just see the usual family fallout – broken crisps, rotten apple cores, discarded parking tickets and half-digested Smarties. I scowl, pump up the volume on my retro 70s punk CD and glare out of the window to the sound of *2-4-6-8 Motorway*. I'm not trucking on through the night, I'm going nowhere. So, as my body stands still, my mind begins to wander. Is this punishment? Is this a sign from God? Is he up there with a megaphone yelling – 'Go home Dave. What are you doing sitting on a B road staring up the backside of a cement truck? It'll only end in tears.' Is it punishment from on high? Is God thwarting my plan for salvation? Will the next move be my engine spontaneously combusting and me dragging myself from the burning wreck with my clothes on fire and my head a charred football? I stop thinking about that alternative really quickly, just in case I somehow make it happen.

Jesus' mates were always worried about the old punishment question. 'That blind man? Is he being punished for what he did or what his parents did?' 'That bloke they lowered through the roof? How could you just forgive him like that? Isn't he steeped in sin?'

'What d'you mean blessed are the poor and the grieving and the broken? They're not blessed – they're under God's curse. He's having a go at them, that's why they're sick and sad.'

Where did the all-knowing disciples get this stuff? Why are they so preoccupied with punishment? Ah, well, flip back to the Old Testament and you'll find plenty of crooked characters spouting duff theology: Job's so-called comforters, for a start. Go on: have a look. You might as well, you'll be stuck in traffic for the best part of an hour.

I find myself staring at the quagmire of Job. Smack in the middle of his rotting flesh period. Feeling bad, Job? Lost everything you care about, Job? Well, it's obvious, isn't it? You've been a very bad lad, a man behaving badly. What have you been up to? Give us the low-down. Go on, tell us the sordid details about the nude fantasies and naked fury. Confess it and all your problems will disappear. But Job's mates were clearly wrong. He wasn't under the cosh for being bad, he was suffering because he was good.

In fact, a quick flash of chapter 29 reveals the full picture on this. Job's been out and about helping the poor and the downtrodden, a voice for the voiceless and friend to the strangers. Clearly he must be stopped. Quick, give him a truckload of bad times and get him in a corner with a little homegroup discussing his sin. That'll stop him walking the walk, he'll be doing what everyone else does – just talking the talk. Chat chat chat. Yak yak yak. That's better – keep Job away from the action – he's way too effective. And a quick glance at Job chapter 30 reveals the extent to which life becomes corrupt when good men do nothing.

Jesus has to correct a few urban myths when he steps on the planet. He seems to spend much of his time bigging up the broken and putting down the proud. That rich man? He's gonna struggle getting into heaven, lads. His wallets are so stuffed, he'll never squeeze through the gates.

What you talking about, Jesus? Those bulging pockets are a sign God loves him. Obey God and you'll be happy and healthy. God's on the side of the rich and successful.

Watch the right TV channels and you can still hear the same dodgy theology.

But Jesus shakes his head and wanders over to a local blind man. He's minding his own business, out there looking for cash rather than a cure, but this really is gonna be pay day.

'This blind man you mentioned,' says Jesus, 'well, just to prove a point, I'll sort out his sight problem and show you it ain't got anything to do with sin.'

And he does. And when a disabled guy drops in and spoils his storytelling, Jesus doesn't bat an eyelid. He just gets up, smiles at the guy and forgives his sins.

Forgives his sins! Arbitrarily and with no confession or repentance? Absolutely. Jesus is like that. Seems I'm the one obsessed with sin. Not him. He's obsessed with life and redemption.

This is news to the disciples and me. Whenever I get stuck in the quicksand of sin, I'm terrified of two things – that God will punish me and I'll be found out and exposed for the true fraud I am.

Mind you – Jesus is not soft. He's not afraid to confront power-wielding hypocrites with their obvious malfunctions. He won't back off from a fight whenever two-faced shysters start laying into him. Like the time some church leaders are having a go at him about his dangerous liaisons with the local lowlife. Jesus calls their bluff on the sin front. There they are thinking that they're hunky dory on the sin-scale, cos they've been to the right college, got the right T-shirts and have appointed themselves as the sin-spotters over other people's lives, and Jesus tells a gripping yarn about a wayward sheep and the kind of wild party they throw in heaven when he's brought back to the fold. This leaves the 'sinless' Pharisees out in the cold, cos if they *don't need to repent of their sin* – then neither will they be attending a big party.

Everything's at a standstill now. Cars, lorries, motor-bikes, dogs, wasps: nothing's moving. Any minute now a bit of tumbleweed will skitter by. Some people are even climbing out of their cars and standing around chatting. I wind down the window, not confident enough to actually get out and walk in case there's a sudden miracle and an angel appears and nukes whatever vehicle is holding us up so that everything suddenly moves off again. That thought makes me actually pray for this kind of miracle but I obviously have been driving too fast because there's no angel around to do the business for me.

Instead, there's a group of young execs leaning on the bonnet of the car behind. Three men and a lady. I catch snippets of their conversation about Monday's reports being better than Tuesday's but not as good as Friday's and twice Thursday's. They discuss pitches and profits and trips to Madrid.

They have great suits with a lot of pin stripes, and I feel very inadequate sitting here in my mid-price jeans and brown cord jacket. Okay, so I love this jacket and would feel like a wardrobe door in a suit but that's not the point. I never ever look that sharp and they do it for a living. I'm definitely not getting out of my car. Luckily the music on my CD is retro and cool right now, but the moment anything cheesy comes on I'll be turning that volume right down.

A family of five spills out of the car somewhere up front. Three kids cavort around on the grassy bank. Forty years ago kids used to dress like their parents – pleated skirts and shirts and ties, now it's all baseball caps and boob tubes – nothing's changed then. Or maybe it's the parents dressing like the kids now. The children are the only ones happy about this jam. Freed from their vehicular prison for a while, they laugh and shout and push each other over. I envy their freedom and I wonder if Jesus did too.

The execs behind continue to look young and very powerful. Somehow they've procured styrofoam cups of steaming black coffee from somewhere They bite croissants, talk on mobiles and brush microscopic crumbs from their lapels. They're talking about the top gear currently being awarded for work achievements: laptops and widescreen TVs. They inhabit another planet to me. What would they make of my little black book? Did they grow up with one? Have they ever felt desperate or inspired enough to reach for one? Do they have any idea of the sinners' parties thrown in heaven every so often, every few moments in those particular bits of heaven hovering over Africa or China?

Time stands still and I turn back to my battered black book, being careful not to hold it up too high, just in case I'm spotted for what I am – a moody goat, desperately trying to keep his life under control, scouring his dull days for evidence of an extraordinary God. Sounds grand put like that, doesn't it?

The eponymous widow of this parable might well have been poor and old but she sure hadn't lost her nerve where God was concerned. She ranted and raved and bent his ear. She gave as good as she got, just or unjust she was gonna face up to God and see this one through.

Jesus once again breaks all the rules and starts referring to God as an unjust judge. What! That's not right. He'll get a few letters of complaint after this show. But Jesus ain't that bothered about letters of complaint. He's more concerned about connecting with people – and clearly he understands that we all have days when we think God is unjust and we fear he will judge us. Like today. So I sit in my traffic jam and wait.

12. The Road to Hell

Luke 10:25–37

One day a religious expert turned up to test Jesus.

'Teacher,' he said, 'what must I do to get eternal life?'

Jesus replied, 'What does the law of Moses say? How do you read that?'

The man answered, '"You must love the Lord your God with all your heart, all your soul, all your strength, and all your mind." And, "Love your neighbour as yourself."'

'Right!' Jesus told him. 'There's your answer!'

But the man wanted to justify himself, so he asked Jesus, 'And who's my neighbour?'

Jesus replied with an illustration: 'A Jewish man was travelling from Jerusalem to Jericho, when he was attacked by bandits. They stripped him of his clothes and money, beat him up, and left him half-dead beside the road . . .'

I had a strange dream last night. I'd forgotten it till now. D'you ever get that? Suddenly, from nowhere, in an idle moment of the day you remember dreaming about Scarlett Johansson and a vat of molten chocolate. I won't go into any more details on that one . . . But sitting here now, another dream comes back to haunt me. Must have been all that beer and cheese I swallowed. Last night seems so long ago – back in that land of domestic life, wife and kidsville, a volcanic place full of mountains of toys, washing up, recycling, dirty washing and sticky things my two-year-old has carefully removed from our kitchen bin. In the dream it was night and there was this young guy out with his girlfriend. Not sure where they'd been . . . maybe to the cinema. No idea what they saw. Maybe a road movie. They were driving back, it was midnight, raining, dark . . . I can still see it all now, which is unusual for me.

The boy and the girl leave the cinema, the rain is heavy. They go to the pub next door and time passes in the snap of a finger. They run out to the car, using the free movie mags as cover from the downpour, fumble with the locks, jump inside and drive away.

The boy is driving. The girl is high, draped over the boy, kissing him, playing with his body. He makes feeble attempts to push her off. There is the sound of a car horn as they almost scrape a passing vehicle coming the other way. Suddenly, there is the sound of a louder horn from behind. It blares repeatedly, again and again and again, and the inside of their car is lit up by the powerful head-lights from a vehicle on their tail.

The boy says something like: 'Sheesh! Turn the cackin' lights down, will ya!'

The girl looks round and squints into the glare.

Three men are inside the car behind, two leaning out of the windows shouting. The horn continues to blare at them.

The girl says: 'Do you know them?'

The boy squints into the mirror then shakes his head.

'Probably drunk,' the boy says.

A hand flings an empty bottle from the car behind. It bounces on the roof of their car as the headlights behind begin to flash on and off.

The girl is now sobering up fast. She is scared.

Girl: 'I don't like it, I don't like this. Let them past, Gary, please!'

The first car pulls over and the second pulls wide. Then it screeches to a halt, cutting in on the first car, crunching against the front wing and pinning it against the side of the road.

Boy: 'What the . . . ?'

The boy tries to open the door but it connects with the body of one of the three men now standing outside. A hand appears in the window. There is a click and a blade appears in it. A face appears on the girl's side of the car. The man speaks. He swears and leers at the girl. There are flecks of beer on his chin. His intentions are very bad indeed . . .

My dream fractured at that point. There was a noise outside the window. Half asleep, I stood up, peeled back the curtains and peered outside. There was a ghostly white sheen splashed across our backyard, a siren wailed and a group of kids recited the latest hip hop classic. Something along the lines of 'Flipping put your flipping hands in the flipping air, like you flipping well just don't flipping care.' Except there was very little flipping in it and a lot of . . . well, you know where this is going. More sirens and screaming engines, the kids swore their way off into the distance and out of my life. And the night fell silent again. Cold and still like a grave. I crawled back to my bed and immediately slipped back into the dream.

I shut my eyes and saw a piece of torn clothing lying in the mud by the side of the road. It is still raining heavily. The girl is screaming. There is also the sound of panting. The boy is lying on his side with his face in the mud. There is a dark red patch on his clothes, he is pressing his hand against it and flinching from the pain. The door of the second car is wide open.

One of the men is sitting inside and jabbing the radio search button with the point of the knife, which now has smears of red spattered on it. He stops and listens as it tunes to *My Way* by Sid Vicious. He turns and looks at the girl. Somewhere in the background, someone's laughing.

Her face is lined with the effort of blocking out what's really happening to her. There is a hand pressing her head hard against the bonnet of her car. She is in terrible pain. The sound of the man's grunting continues, then stops. The girl swallows and bites on her lip. There is blood on her mouth.

The men speak to each other. Mutterings about finishing up and getting out of there.

There is the sound of footsteps, a car starts up, doors slam and they drive away.

The music fades. The girl shuts her eyes and painfully raises her head. The road is quiet for about thirty seconds then another car approaches. The girl flinches, thinking that they've come back for another go.

But there's a religious sticker in the back window of this car. A husband and wife argue inside. She is annoyed with him because he has accepted a cut in pay. Suddenly he sees a figure in the road, slams on the brakes and leans out of the window, shouting: 'Get out of the road!'

The girl is standing there, only half dressed, her clothes torn; she has flagged them down.

Girl: 'Please, you gotta help, we've been attacked . . .'

The husband and wife look over at the car skewed off the road. The wife shakes her head.

Wife: 'Kids . . .'

The husband leans out again.

Husband: 'I'm sorry, we're late.'

As the girl continues to shout to them, they pull away and drive round her.

She drops onto her knees, sobbing and screaming.

Half a mile away, another car approaches. The driver is a man alone, Radio 3 playing in the background. He passes a black Mercedes, parked by the side of the road.

Two heads appear over the top of the Mercedes and both suddenly grin, urchin-like. A fist wrapped in a rag punches through the car window. There is the sound of a car alarm. The doors slam shut, a CD is shoved in the player and the car pulls away, the sound of Eminem blasting out.

Back in the Radio 3 car, the driver plucks a sandwich from a plastic carton, turns a corner and takes a bite, losing a wad of tuna and sweetcorn as his teeth tear at the thick white bread. As he chews, he hears an engine rev behind him. It's the Mercedes.

The two joyriders are laughing and shouting, passing a bottle between the two of them as neither of them controls the car.

Joyrider: 'Take him! Take him! Burn him up!'

The man in the car in front looks in his mirror and sees the joyriders closing on him fast. The joyriders pull wide to overtake, both cars filling the width of the road.

Joyrider: 'Wotchit!'

They all see the girl at the same time, still kneeling in the road, sobbing and screaming, her face contorted like a Halloween mask. Both cars slam the brakes on. The man swerves and catches the girl with his rear wing, throwing her to one side. The joyriders' car spins round and comes to rest on the verge. The Radio 3 man looks back, sees the girl lying in the road, panics and drives on. The two joyriders leap out, their bottle smashing on the road, and run over to the girl.

Joyrider: 'You all right?'

The girl is dazed but manages to stand up.

Girl : 'I . . . I've been . . . raped . . .'

The last word comes out as a sob.

The two joyriders look at each other then stare at the disappearing car.

Girl: 'My boyfriend . . . He's half dead.'

They look over at the boy, lying face down.

The two joyriders drag the boy through the slew of water and mud towards their car. The girl limps after them. She can barely make it across the road and collapses over the boot. They pull the boy to the car and open the back door. One of them climbs in and hauls the body inside. The girl falls in after them.

They drive away and pull up at a hospital. The kids don't hang around. The girl pulls the boy out and drags him towards the reception desk.

As the dream faded a question echoed in my head.

'So – here's a question for you – which of them do you think showed any love?'

I shudder from the memory and glance over at the passenger door. It's unlocked. They're all unlocked. I'm on a busy road in broad daylight and I'm a regular guy. I'm not scared. Why should I be? I lock it. I lock 'em all, only temporarily, but the dream has spooked me. It's the old traffic accident effect – most people slow down for a while after witnessing a car wreck. So I lock the door, very aware that violence is not just the stuff of nightmares and movies. Why did I have to dream that? Why? Why? It leaves a foul taste in my soul. I turn the music up but it won't drown out the images. I turn it down again. We're still not moving.

Jesus told such searing tales. I've seen a hundred picture books of smiling Samaritans in stripy dressing gowns casually bundling smiling injured victims onto the back of soft furry smiling donkeys. A million miles from the yarn Jesus spun. Bandits mugging travellers still happens today, it's sickening and terrifying, backpackers and car-jack victims can end up dead. You wouldn't expect JK Rowling to turn that sort of brutal crime into a glossy kids' tale. And another thing, the whole meaning of Samaritan has morphed. They're smiley happy caring people now. The epitome of the listening ear. These days, if we're depressed, we call 'em up: back then, they used to beat 'em up. Samaritans weren't on the end of a phone, they were on the end of your fist. They were hated and feared – rather like the members of al-Qaeda today. Jesus' tale would have left a bad taste, the kind of bad taste I'm struggling with now.

13. Angry Young Men

John 7:1–13; John 2:1–12; Luke 11:37–54

After this, Jesus moved around Galilee for a while. He didn't go to Judea for a while because the Jews had secretly put out a contract on him. But the Feast of Tabernacles was looming so his brothers got him in a corner one day and said to him, 'You should go into Judea to the festival so that your disciples can see the things you're doing. If you want to be famous, there's no point hiding here. If you're gonna change the world, get out there and do something and let everyone know about it.' This from the guys who recently tried to get him locked up for antisocial behaviour. They were just provoking him because, having grown up together, they were not really convinced by him.

Jesus said to them, 'Don't force me, guys, you know me, we've had this out before. I'll do things in my own time. You can do things your own way but my hands are tied. I can't move around freely, there's a curfew on my life. I've spoken too freely and I've provoked the author-ities. What they do is clearly evil. But they don't want to hear that and I'm in trouble for pointing it out. You guys go up to the feast, I'll stay away this time. Maybe next year. Have a great time.'

Of course this really didn't satisfy them but he was adamant so they left him in Galilee. But after his brothers had gone to the feast then he went himself, not publicly, but in secret . . .

'Mother – give me a break!'

Weddings can be stressful at the best of times, but if you've under-catered, then the party's over. Things are about to turn extremely pomegranate-shaped. So Mary consults her eldest boy.

'This is your moment! Do something! Go on! You can do this – it's your chance to shine!'

'Look, don't push me, mum, I'm not sure this is a good idea.'

'Go on. Look how many people are here. They need the wine. There'll be a lot of red faces without it.'

'There'll be a lot of red faces with it.'

Jesus shrugs and goes to get some space. Mary goes to the groom.

'Trust me,' she says, 'whatever he suggests, it'll work.'

On his way out, Jesus spots six huge jars of water and an idea sneaks into his mind. He glances skywards for a moment. No sign up there, no guidance written in the clouds. But something in his spirit clicks. Perhaps this is his time after all. He stops and takes a deep breath. If he does this, nothing will be the same again. This is the start of everything. He rubs a nervous hand across his forehead.

'Are you all right?'

It's Andrew.

Jesus smiles at him. 'Yea,' he says, 'hang onto your sandals: the party's about to start for real.'

Jesus beckons to a couple of servants and the rest, as they say, is history . . .

'You didn't wash your hands.'

'I know.'

The Pharisee frowns. 'You know?'

'Yes.'

'So do it.'

'Why?'

'Because it's the word of God.'

'Oh really?'

'Yes, you should know that.'

'I'll tell you what I know. You can wash your hands and your face and your plates and cups till the sheep come home: it won't change a thing. If you want to be clean – sluice out your spirit. You may smell great on the outside but you're foul on the inside. You wanna get clean? Care for the poor. Look out for them. Lift up the downtrodden. Stand up for the oppressed. Stop making demands on people – the kind of demands you'll never keep yourself. Believe me, if you start caring for others, you'll be as clean as you ever need to be. At the moment, you're about as clean as an open sewer.'

I'm going nowhere. I've done one mile in the last hour. Anyway you slice it, that's one mile an hour. Jeremy Clarkson would be laughing his Formula One socks off. I can feel the road rage building up again. This is worse than being in church. Or if not worse, then very similar.

Jammed into a confined space unable to move about. No control, no means of fighting back. Having to do what you're told. Sit there and shut up. Takes me back to school where I first met Joel. I rebelled against it then and not much has changed. Sometimes I sit in church, less often these days, but sometimes I'm there, shoehorned in one of those cramped hard pews, my blood boiling at what this faith has become. So much of church is irrelevant and downright weird.

I do believe the church is alive and well, but I'm not convinced that what we think of as church is what God thinks is church. 'And I say to you that you are Peter, and on this rock I will build my church and the gates of hell, conformity, boredom or mundanity will not prevail against her.'

When Jesus said that, I very much doubt this action man imagined rows and rows of people singing songs and listening to lectures.

People say there's great meaning and power in the old ritual and symbolism. All that received gilt-edged wisdom from the old days. And sure I'm the first to stick my hand up and say I love a bit of visual inducement and sensory stimulation. But if the symbolism doesn't work ... what's the point? It's no good doing stuff that we then have to explain, there's no purpose speaking a language that requires a blinkin' Christian-to-English dictionary. Jesus' jokes, yarns and daring doing slapped people round the face and struck them in the gut. It made them gasp and laugh and cry and shout. We still do a lot of stuff now that would have got that reaction a hundred years back – but those old saints are long gone. There's nothing spiritual about speaking in a way no one connects with any more. Everything in my little battered Bible was once contemporary. Let's keep it that way.

Fed up and festering, I pick up my mobile and finally report in.

My wife and I have a clipped snappy conversation with a lot of one-word answers and very little humour. We can't see each other but I think we both know neither is smiling. She was in a good mood before I called. She was having a good time, then I dialled up and complained about my thwarted escape attempt. I switch the phone off, sigh and grab my little black book. As I angrily thumb the pages, I tear a few and crease lots of others. Well, at least she knows where I am now, even if my confession of being AWOL makes neither of us very happy. Perhaps I should have just called in sick, phoned up and feigned hepatitis B

or something. Mind you she might then have come surg-
ing back to me with the kids in tow. And we wouldn't
want that.

It's not that I don't want to be married, it's just that I
don't want to be married for these three days. I sigh
again and try to repair the damaged pages of my little
black book. My eyes fall on a passage about Jesus on a
bad day. So he knows how I feel then.

There is a prevailing and popular notion that if you
are a very good person then God will really like you,
and if you lived 2K years back Jesus would have put you
in his gang, or posse, or triad or whatever you want to
call it. Likewise, if you're in a foul mood and feel like
breaking a window he won't like you.

Load of old rubbish.

The people in Jesus' triad were losers, wasters, control
freaks and bullies. The kind of people your mother
warned you about. Twelve angry men and seventy-two
lost souls.

Next time you're sitting around with a fag and a brew,
or a pint and a curry, re-read one of the Gospels (tackle
Mark – it's short) and try to do it as if you have never
read it before. Maybe you haven't, in which case you
won't have to do the trying bit.

If you have read it already, throw your head to the skies
and send up a silent plea that you'll be able to see this thing
with new eyes. I'm told that the original Gospels were written in *common* Greek – the language of the people – not
some high religious vernacular but street-speak. The same
language used for shopping lists and first-century post-it
notes. The early journalists got these hot stories down in
words of two syllables, words everyone could understand.
Tramps and hobos, hippies and rock stars; the up-and-
coming and the down-and-out. They put it out in the *Daily
Mirror* rather than the *Daily Telegraph*.

I glance out the window and see that I'm being over-taken by a slug. He's on a leaf in a nearby hedge and unlike me, he's crawling somewhere. I feel the road rage rising again.

Three things make me angry – no, four – bullies, my inability to be James Bond, traffic jams and church. Church, church, church. Nothing makes me see red quite so much as enforced happiness on a Sunday morning. My guess is that synagogue made Jesus mad too. Whenever he went, he caused a hell of a stink. Organised religion wasn't used to the presence of God. It's too messy, too provocative, too real.

Jesus wasn't a stained-glass saint – and these aggressive encounters I'm surfing through prove the point. His brothers just didn't get him. Had he ever been close to them? Maybe they were too close: family can breed contempt. He was clearly the older brother – so was he much older, a distant figure perhaps? Then one day he steps out of the shadows covered in sand, renounces the family business and starts waxing on about the kingdom of God. What would you make of it if your brother or cousin or uncle suddenly started on like that?

And then there's his mum, his dear old mum who'd long lived with a sword in her soul, knowing who her oldest boy really was. Is she frustrated? Has she seen too little of the divine in her lad as he played with the other kids and then learnt the family business from his dad? He's spent years making tables and benches – when is he gonna do something? Has the sword begun to rankle inside, is it digging into her heart with impatience?

'Don't push me, ma, I'm a big boy now. I need to think for myself.'

Jesus seems to be on his own journey of discovery. He needs to hear from his Father about the use of miracles, not his mother. He wanders off alone, escapes the noise and the bustle and the music and dancing. And then, humility clutched in both hands, he returns to do his mother's bidding. It is a good idea after all. And the same happens with his brothers, they're egging him on, pushing him to go to the shindig – but he's not sure. And then he goes in secret. But by then he's more mature anyway; maybe he knows that going in secret is much the best way. *Don't* want the circus to come to town the moment he arrives at the feast. News travels fast and he wouldn't be able to move for the paparazzi if he went with the family. He needs to go covertly, in the shadows, so he can actually get a few things done. Jesus doesn't want to be famous: fame corrodes your soul and blinds your vision – and without vision people die.

Did he often argue with his brothers? And being the Son of God, did he always win? He certainly frequently left the Pharisees fuming in a pool of their own frustration. At times it almost seems as if they conduct a slanging match. They call him possessed, he calls them dead men. They call him blasphemous, he calls them hypocrites. They accuse him of mixing with scum, he accuses them of vanity and greed. And it goes on. And on. And on. Jesus won't pull his punches. They go at it hammer and tongues. No wonder he upset them. He jabbed a finger in their direction and hit the naked truth button. They were very good at obeying the man-made rules – but they were bottom of the league when it came to knowing what God really wanted. Whores and crooks were closer to God than they were.

I think about Jesus in his Father's house. Anger spilling out of him, the divine Temple raider, so angry that he started throwing furniture about. Apparently that bit of the Temple he trashed was for Gentiles – a place where the whole world could meet God. He wasn't gonna have it turned into the Royal Bank of Israel.

Mammon had ousted the Maker: well the Maker was back, and big time. The meek and mild one is standing there with spit on his beard and fire in his face – yelling about thieves and cheats and desecration.

So what about my anger? Sitting here in this car yelling at myself about cars and churches that are both going nowhere. Is my fury justified? I daren't think about it. I probably have more in common with Jonah than Jesus. It got right up his nose when God didn't wipe out a bunch of miserable sinners, but he redirected his anger at a poor old plant that had done nothing wrong. Dumping my traffic temper all over my missus is not really a good idea – but then I'm a past master at dumping all over the family. Bad day at work? Intimidated on the way home? Not enough money in the bank? Got the hots for someone else? Jealous and insecure? Don't panic – just take it all out on the ones you love.

Another sigh and I close my Bible. I hope this traffic moves soon or I might break a window.

14. The Difference between In-laws and Outlaws

Exodus 18:13–27

Moses has a straight-talking father-in-law. Jethro's about to pay him a visit in the desert and if his daughter's anything to go by, then he's very probably a no-nonsense kind of guy. When Moses was umming and ahhing about whether to hack off their son's foreskin, she waded in with the meat cleaver and adopted the circumcision position. Well, now her old man Jethro's here, knocking on the tent flap and asking to see the guy in charge.

'Hey Mo, how's it going?'

'Well, apart from nearly being slaughtered, then nearly drowning and now nearly starving – we're doing really well. And don't call me Mo. I'm supposed to be respected round here.'

'So I heard Mo, is that why you've got a long line of moaners outside your tent?'

'Yea, and it looks like you jumped the queue, they won't be happy.'

And as if on cue, a face appears through the gap in the tent.

'He jumped the queue!'

'He's family! Respect my family!'

The face disappears, Jethro slaps Moses on the shoulder.

'Mo, take a break. Take a walk. Come on, we can slip out the back.'

Leadership's tough. Especially if you've not commanded an entire nation before.

'They look to me for everything,' says Moses. 'I didn't ask for this.'

'Yea, but natural leadership just leaks out. If it's in there, the dogs come sniffing around you. These people know you have clout. You got the aroma of the Big Man about you, Mo.'

'Well, it's too much.'

'Too right, it's too much. Back off. Delegate!'

'I can't! I'm the leader.'

'That's not what I heard. I heard it was you and Aaron.'

Moses frowns. 'I know, I asked for that initially. But if you want something doing . . .'

'Sure, do it yourself. And die before thirty.'

'That's unlikely. I'm 81.'

'Mo, listen. You're not the only leader round here. There are hundreds, and if you don't use them pretty soon they'll get bored. And then there'll be trouble, cos if you ain't got time to see everyone, everyone'll start looking to the other leaders. So bring 'em all in to your net. Get all the bosses together, brief 'em, oversee 'em and let them do what they're good at. Don't try and do it all. You should oversee your generals. No one else. Let the leaders deal with the man on the street, or the sand in your case. Trust me, I know what I'm saying.'

'Jethro – give me a break.'

'I am giving you a break. It's exactly what I'm giving you.'

When Jethro's gone, Moses takes a lonely stroll up into the dunes. What's a guy to do? He knows his old man-in-law is right but he's miffed that the guy had to come all this way just to tell him how to run his life. He doesn't need advice. Moses has just freed an entire nation, for God's sake. Quite literally. Why should he need some old fella with a cough and a limp come telling him to do a bit of delegation?

Moses scoops up a handful of hot sand and lets it run through his fingers. Down below the line of moaners snakes back through the camp. It's long and getting longer. Moses feels tired just looking at it. He can hear the grumbling from up here.

Moses never thought of himself as a control freak but now that he takes a long hard look back . . . When Egyptian soldiers were suppressing Israelites he tried to wipe 'em out on his own. When God showed up with a master plan, he came up with every reason why he shouldn't go. When God gave him Aaron, he then did it on his own anyway. And now Jethro pops up with good advice that he just wants to toss in the trash can. You need to be humble, Moses, he tells himself. You need to swallow that great wad of pride that sticks in your throat when people offer you a better way. That's the problem with being a survivor. You learn to get by on your own, so living with other people is tough. Moses is so used to doing it his way that rethinking is hard for him. Especially when the advice comes from the in-laws.

Moses recalls that day at the well, fighting off a bunch of ragged shepherds to make a way for Jethro's girls. He decked a couple of the shepherds, kicked a few buckets and yelled a lot and fortunately that was enough to make the others back off. He didn't expect to inherit a family as a result, but the girl's father welcomed him with open arms and before he knew it, he had a wife, a mother-in-law, six sisters and a lot of sheep. His life was suddenly full of females. The first year was particularly difficult and the memories still haunt him now. He did his best to get along with everyone but seven sisters say a lot and you don't always agree . . .

I kid myself I have no idea why I suddenly ran away like this, but now I'm on the road I realise there were a million reasons brewing up in the background. Bubble, bubble, so much trouble. A ticking bomb, or rather an idling engine just waiting for me to put my foot on the accelerator and drive. Not big things, you understand, just a million tiny smudges spoiling the view. Take Dullington Manor for example . . .

Ah! A miracle! The traffic starts to move at long last. I pull away, stall, swear, stall and finally get going. It's been so long since I did any driving I've forgotten how. Where was I? Oh yea, Dullington Manor. It's the kind of place you visit with your in-laws. Expansive lawns full of manicured grass and unpronounceable flowers. A whacking great house full of smelly costumes and old cutlery. An extortionately expensive shop full of tea towels, kids' colouring books and stuff for gardening. (It's so overpriced I once heard a customer say to the girl on the till: 'Dick Turpin wore a mask.') It's just the kind of place you run from screaming in your dreams. Except you'd never go there in your dreams, you go there in real life and no way are you allowed to run out of there screaming, it would upset the flowers. And anyway, there are signs everywhere warning you to keep quiet and not offend anyone. What's the difference between in-laws and outlaws? You guessed it – outlaws are wanted. Dullington Manor advertises itself as a day in heaven. Well, the only similarity I can see is that a day in Dullington Manor can seem like a thousand years. It's

like an hour looking after a two-year-old. Feels like forever. As Romeo and Juliet found to their cost, when two
star-crossed lovers get together they each come with
their own cast of extras. Sometimes it's like trying to
combine the Waltons and the Simpsons and it's no mean
achievement.

The traffic's thinning out now, my foot's on the pedal
and I'm pushing forty-five. (That's in speed, not age.)
I'm starting to feel free again. The Boomtown Rats start
screaming about Rat Traps and breaking out of them and
things look better already. A Land Cruiser burns me off
as it zooms by me in a fat-spare-tyre hurry to be somewhere. I don't care: I'm just in a hurry to be nowhere.
And we're finally getting there. The kids, the washing-
up, the recycling, the work, the debts, the regrets, the
hoovering, the interrupted nights, the early wake-up
calls, the late night tidying up, the phone call to my wife,
even Dullington Manor and the in-laws – they all start to
fall away. I can almost look back and see a trail of my life
strewn back there behind me on the road. If I drive for
long enough, it'll all be gone. I could start my life again
and just be someone else. Anyone else. Nothing can stop
me. Nothing. I'm a rocket ship on my way to . . . Oh
great. Another hold-up. The traffic quickly thickens and
we all go from fifty to zero in about thirteen seconds.
Before you can say Michael Schumacher, I'm crunching
the gears and grinding my teeth again. Visions of
Dullington come crashing back round me just as Bobby
G screams about being caught in that same old rat trap,
just when you thought you were getting free.

Did Moses feel trapped when his father-in-law
showed up? Did it bring back memories of Zipporah's
feisty sisters? Did he fully expect to see his mother-in-
law out the back, arm-wrestling a couple of bears? Or
breathing on manna and making toast? If not trapped,

then he probably felt inhibited by Jethro, his style may well have been cramped. But he did well to listen. We men are excellent at doing our own thing. Senor Sinatra summed it up so well when he crooned about his way. And how popular is that tune? Genghis Khan, Josef Stalin, Nero. How they would have loved that little number. Thankfully Moses never heard Frankie, he just listened to Jethro, opened his portable ice box and pulled out a huge slab of humble pie.

15. The Bad Sex Guide

2 Samuel 13:1–19

Amnon spends a lot of time on his own these days. He mooches in fields, stares at sunsets and he's always in the kitchen at parties. He's not eating properly, not much at all in fact, he's wasting away and Jonadab has noticed. Jonadab's no fool, he's Amnon's cousin and a good friend of the family.

'What's up, mate?'

He sidles up one day and steals a spot on the wall beside Amnon, as he wishes away another hour staring at the sun.

'A girl.'

'Ah. Sure. Girls. Do I know her?'

'I should think so, she's your cousin.'

Jon thinks for a minute, considers the possibilities and eliminates the usual suspects.

'So that'll be . . .' He gives a low whistle. 'You've got good taste, mate. A little unorthodox, but good taste nonetheless.'

'For all the good it'll do me. I'll be dead before it comes to anything.'

'Not necessarily.'

Amnon rips his eyes from the sun and frowns at his friend.

'What d'you mean?' he asks.

'Well, you're clearly under the weather, aren't you? No appetite, no energy, no focus. Exploit that. Make the most of it. Struggle to your sick bed and plead serious illness. Obviously nothing contagious. Something that a little bit of TLC will sort out. Female TLC. Know what I mean, nudge nudge wink wink.'

Amnon sighs. He does a lot of sighing these days.

'I could try it,' he says.

'Do it! Don't try. Ask your old man for your sister's help. Get him to get her to bring you some cookies. She makes great cookies. And when you're alone – and make sure you end up alone – wham bam thank you Tamar. Easy.'

Jon spreads his hands and grins. For the first time in months Amnon grins too. They give each other five. The pact is sealed. It might just work.

It doesn't. Oh, it gets her into bed, and Amnon has his wicked way and sows his wild oats. Gets to see her the way he's always wanted to, but as soon as it's over there's no joy. No satisfaction. This isn't the way of his dreams. He just feels sick inside. And she looks small and white and not the girl he thought she was. She stands by his bed now, trembling and naked and sobbing. What's he done? What has he done? The horror fills his head and self-loathing creeps like freezing fog from his loins to his heart. It was so quick and so cruel. Nothing's been accomplished and he waited so long for it. He has a fleeting moment in which to decide what to do. He makes another bad choice.

'Get out!' he snarls. 'Get out of here, whore, you should never have come.'

'But you asked for me. Don't be like this.'

She stops crying and looks him in the eye.

'Marry me, Amnon. It doesn't have to turn out bad. We'll talk to Dad.'

'What are you talking about? It's already turned out bad. You're not beautiful at all. You've used me.'

He can't get the fear of God out of him. What if he's found out?

She says something but she's crying again and her voice is clogged with so much emotion, he has to yell at her to repeat it.

She sobers up again. 'I said if you don't have me, no one will. I'll die alone and bitter. And all because you violated me.'

'I did not. Get out, you stupid slut. You suckered me into this. I don't love you, I never did. Get out and don't come back. And don't tell David!'

And Tamar leaves, she gathers her clothes and is still pulling them on as she goes through the door, leaving her half-brother contemplating how easily he let his manhood rule his mind. For a while there he confused his groin with his grey matter. He won't do that again in a hurry.

In many ways this is the antithesis of Solomon's good sex guide. This is a bad sex guide. And it proves that the Bible won't shy away from the hard things in life. This portrays the empty destructive side of lust. The top shelf, back alley, red light, wham bam and shove off mam guide to getting your socks off just to lionise your loins. The 'buy now pay later' offer.

Although in Amnon's case he's not buying, he's stealing. A cloud comes over him and before he knows it he's consumed with lust for Tamar. She's in his head all the time. He can't eat, can't sleep, can't work. He feels sick every day. Every girl he sees, he thinks it's her. Every fantasy in his head is all about her. The moment he crosses the line is unclear, but at some point he switches off the fantasy channel and starts hatching real plans,

plans to get her out of his head and into his bed. Her firm young body fills his imagination all day now. This is gonna be the best thing that ever happened to him.

This is dangerous territory.

The university of lust.

Thinking with your groin instead of your brain.

A cloud came over me recently. Another little reason for running away. The most perfect girl in the world came to temp in our office. We had everything in common, same movies, same music, same jokes, same frustrations. Where had we been all our lives? We were made for each other. Till I volunteered to take her on a two-hour trip to catch a plane. Suddenly we had nothing in common. She came from the planet Weird. I didn't like her at all. By the end of the journey I wanted to kill her. What was I thinking of? I drove back from that airport feeling like an idiot. And when she came back to work a week later I acted like one. Could barely look at her without flinching, couldn't speak to her, didn't know what to say. Movies, music, jokes – so what? When I said I was interested in all those things, what I really meant was all her other bits. The obvious ones. And I'm not talking about her manicured nails or fine bone structure. The spirit of Amnon lurks in the corner of every man's life. Sin crouches, winking at us, nudging us, waiting for those moments when it can move in and take up residence.

Now, driving away from it all today, I see it all so clearly, but back there, steeped in stupidity, I didn't have a clue.

I find this such a searing tale; brutal, cowardly, horrific – yet it's one I relate to so easily. Using women for your own end. Mentally, emotionally, physically, whichever. Then despising them and wishing they were on another planet.

Amnon makes me shudder. What he did was appalling, and it's too much like looking in a mirror. Okay, so I didn't force her to make brownies and feed them to me, I didn't grab her wrist and tear off her clothes, but in my head? How often? How often? And how many other women? The problem with us guys is we see something and want it. Now. Whether in the flesh or on the net. Our eyes go out on stalks and our brain goes into sleep mode. We can go from 0 to 60 in the time it takes to say *cold shower*. We are visually stimulated, or shallow, if you're a woman. I won't even begin to sum up the female species, only to say this, men and women are different. And it would be better if hormones came with body armour.

The more pointless crushes I have, the more it makes me realise I married the right girl. And I guess that sounds like a backhanded compliment. Someone told me that a man can fall in love seven times after getting married. Seven times? Seven!? And the rest. Seventy times seven more like. I frequently go up and down that roller coaster of lerve and always end up dizzy and sick from the ride. But I still come back for more. Maybe I watch too many movies that tell me that love is a cardiac event that makes your temperature rise and your head spin. But they're just confusing it with a bad case of flu.

Mind you it's not all bad – some of those cardiac events are with the girl of my dreams, I frequently fall in and out of love with the one I put on a penguin suit and shiny shoes for – now that is dedication. 'Getting married sir? Step right this way, we've got your clown outfit right here.'

Falling in love's easy: I can do it with my eyes shut – and I often do. Commitment: that's the uncharted water, the impossible mission, the last mountain, the temple of doom.

So many of us settle for the quick fix, the one-night stand, the fast and furious *How's your old man* and then Ciao! and move on. That's the thing about perpetually new love – it's not really true love, it's just convenient.

And every tale of rejection in my little black book, and there are many in here, only serves to remind me that the God of heaven talks a very different language. The one whose eyes burn like a furnace, the one whose love is fierce and frank and forever.

How many times has God humiliated himself in his search for love? How many times has he looked the fool? We jump headlong into a lifelong relationship with him, claiming devotion and commitment, but he can see in our eyes that we're thinking *One night stand, one night stand*. But he never gives up. Instead he looks for the guys who will make his point for him.

'Hosea – you're gonna get married, mate. And she's a real looker. The problem is everyone else will think so too – and she'll be in other people's beds more often than yours. It'll break your heart and smack your self-confidence. But everywhere you go, people will know – this is the guy who won't give up on love. This is the foolish guy who'll wait forever.'

16. You Can Run but You Can't Hide

Psalm 139

O Lord, you have examined my heart, my mind and my soul and know everything about me.

You know when I sit down or stand up. You know my every thought when far away.

You chart the path ahead of me and you know when I need to stop and rest.

You know every moment of the day where I am.

You know what I am going to say before the words are out of my mouth.

You're in front of me, behind me, above me, beside me. You place your hand of blessing on my head.

This knowledge blows my mind. It's too difficult for me to get my head around.

It's too much to absorb. I hear myself say the words but they don't really go in.

There is nowhere I can go where you have not been. No situation too bad, no experience too dark. You're there ahead of me all the time. I can never escape from your spirit! I can never get away from you!

If I go up to heaven, you are there; paradise or the underworld, you're all over the place. You fill the universe. Even the dead of night is not dead or night to you. You're like a blind man when the lights are off – the darkness makes no difference to you whatsoever.

I could plead for death but I'd find you waiting. You've been there from my birth – from conception. You designed me, you wired me up, you assembled my DNA and made me unique, complex and individual. There's no one like me, Lord and there's no one like you.

I could tell you where this place is but I'll let you decide, let it be your dream place in your dream bit of England. I pull in through the gate, tyres crunching on the proverbial sweeping gravel drive. I draw up near the front door and park on the concrete forecourt.

I love this place. I've only ever been here three times but it seems like a bit of heaven. Maybe because I've only ever been here three times. Nothing sullies it. It's green and large and full of space and time. No sign of my friend though. My dear long-lost school buddy – where the hell is he? It's bang on five, why isn't he standing here waiting to greet me with arms open wide and a bottle of whiskey in his hand?

I circle the building a few times, soaking up the silence and gazing up at the empty grey windows beneath that perfect blue sky.

It's an old Georgian farmhouse, three floors and four acres. Joel bought it with a stack of money left to him by an old aunt. We first met at school, went separate ways and became the best of friends. He's had several wives, no kids and loves languages and shooting. We're oceans apart in many ways yet often find ourselves in the same boat; usually a little old dinghy with both oars missing and a slow puncture just above the waterline. Joel's taller, thinner and better-looking than me, but I think he envies my stability and family. Strange that, seeing I've pitched up hankering after his freedom and bachelor lifestyle. Ah, the words *greener* and *grass* come to mind, not necessarily in that order. I like the little things we do, walking in the nearby beech-lined park, carting gargan-tuan lumps of wood over, going to see movies that are both terrible and inadvertently hilarious. I like all that stuff. It's not conquering the world on BMWs or taking twenty-six men to the South Pole but it's what makes our friendship what it is.

A car horn barges into my consciousness and I turn to see Joel pulling in through the gates, a look of complete bewilderment on his face. Perhaps I should have rung ahead.

The reunion is warm and awkward, as is often the case with us. We talk too quickly and make very little sense. I feel disorientated from so much driving. So we stand outside for a while, drinking fresh air, staring at the view and avoiding too much eye contact. We get cold and Joel makes us tea and I eventually feel I'm begin-ning to leave the inside of the car behind. Thawing out from journeys always takes me a good while. I crack open the jaffa cakes and we wolf the lot down between us. Joel says something about firewood so I follow him across the vast lawn towards a woodshed. I watch him swing an axe and split a few logs for the fire, feeling slightly less of a man than him cos he's got a big chop-per and I haven't.

Joel brings in a huge pile of logs and sets about burning them in the huge fireplace at one end of the large sitting room. At the other end, beyond the huge bay window, the sun begins to set and the sky turns golden and wistful as the evening sets the stage for another autumn night. The logs fizz and split and crack and we pull up a couple of beanbags and slouch by the fire. That's better, life's begin-ning to feel good again.

Like *Withnail and I* we sit around for a while trying to get warm and swigging a variety of ill-advised drinks. We loosen up, laugh and talk like men who are somewhat out of control. That's what friends are for.

We sit by the fire for a long time, watching the logs spew flame and spit sparks, chatting about the old days and what we're up to now.

I guess if anyone knows me well, it's Joel. I don't easily let out what I'm really thinking. Most of the times only God knows, and boy did he make me fearfully complex. As Joel takes a call from his friend Mike-the-Bike, I fish out my Bible and read Psalm 139. I don't think I've indulged in so much extreme Bible study all my born days, and I probably won't do again. This page of David's blog both warms my soul and scares the living Bible out of me. I can't get away from God. I can drive for miles and leave everything behind – except him and me. I can try and be holy, try and put on a brave face, try and think the right things and say the right words – but he knows. I often catch myself trying to pray the right prayers in just the right way, attempting to somehow cover up my real desires and fears. Then I stand up and relax and it's as if I catch him tapping me on the shoulder saying, 'Oi! I'm still here, you know.'

Try as I might, there's nothing I can conceal from the One who made eyes and understanding, but I'm trying to get it into my dull skull that he's not snooping – he's interested. This twisted, frayed life of mine all matters to him. My foibles, my choices, my frustrations and temptations, even my desire to flee for a few days. I can't escape the God of freedom because he's too tolerant; he's patient enough to walk with me every single day, on and on along the meandering route that is my life. He'll sit it out with me here at Joel's for as long as it takes for me to get my head back together.

Like I said, reassuring and scary.

17. Blinded by the Light

Mark 9:2–27

'So what are we doing up here then, Lord?'

Peter kicks at a nearby rock, he rolls it to John, John kicks it back. James joins in and they boot the little boulder back and forth for a while.

Then they realise Jesus hasn't replied to the question.

They glance over and get the shock of their lives. He's smiling at them but his face is lit with the glow of a thousand torches. They squint to keep looking at him; the light's travelling down his body, over his chest and his pelvis on down through his legs to his feet. His whole body's on fire, but it's not burning up, and the light is white, pure eyeball-melting white. The guys hold their palms in front of their faces and peek over their fingers

They hear steps and turn to see two more figures coming up the mountain. But these aren't more travellers, they're lit up too like a forest fire. They stop when they see Jesus and make their way over. John and James glance at each other. What's going on?

The whole mountain is shot through with light and warmth now. Peter starts laughing.

'You know what this is?' he says. 'This is what we've been waiting for. This is what he's always bashing on about. This is the kingdom. See that guy with the staff – what d'you reckon? Moses? And the other one – Aaron?

Soon they'll all be here. This place will be full of the prophets. You won't be able to move for beards and staffs. This is the end.'

James isn't laughing. 'The end of what?' he says.

'The end of the journey. Heaven's coming down – look, see the cloud. We're gonna be here forever. Our troubles are over! Hey Jesus? Where d'you want your tent, mate? We can nip down and bring everything up here. We can get tents for all of us. This is brilliant. Hey! And guess what? Thomas isn't here! He'll be livid. He'll be going sheep-dung down there!'

Peter rubs his hands and laughs again.

It's not Aaron with Moses. It's Elijah, the bi-polar prophet who struggled so much. He and the brutally honest Moses are standing in this soda stream of light talking and laughing with Jesus. And Jesus looks more relaxed than he has for months. It seems as if meeting with these guys has changed something. Suddenly there's a crack of thunder from above. Thunder – but no lightning, and as the sound rumbles on words meld with the booming.

'This is my Son. Listen to him. Take good note of what he tells you.'

A thick cloud falls on everyone and suddenly Peter's not laughing any more. It's so thick they can't see their hands in front of their faces and Jesus and the prophets have completely disappeared. Peter wades around in the fog, grasping at the wisps of cloud for something else human. His finger jabs James in the eye and the other man cusses.

'James! James! What's going on?'

'You're blinding me, that's what's going on. Get away from me!'

The cloud lifts as quickly as it fell and they turn to see Jesus, looking more like the way they remember him. No

lights, no booming thunder, no prophets. But something
about him is different.

I love the early evening light there at this time of year, a
sort of thick, dry, autumnal glaze, it breaks over the cottage lawn like the glow from a giant desk lamp, it's all
kind of white and orange and golden and magical.
Warms your soul and lights your mind. I almost expect
Clint Eastwood and Kevin Costner to come riding over
the horizon shouting and hollering as they chase wild
steer and masked outlaws, waving their revolvers in the
air.

The place doesn't really have a back garden, it just sits
in the middle of so much greenery refusing to engage
with the world and its madness. I stand by the door for
a while, watching the dying glow and feeling the slow
warmth on my face. There's a cool breeze too. A gentle
Indian summer whisper. Almost like the breath of God.

Can I stay here forever, Lord?

Not likely, mate. Course you can't. Like Jesus up the
mountain, you're here for some R&R. Time out. This is a
shot in the arm and a boot up the backside to get you in
shape and back out there again.

Shame, Lord. Be nice to move in and stay for a few
years.

What was Jesus doing up that mountain? And why?

Did God show him an inventory of A-list biblical guys
and say 'Pick a couple of friends, you can have anyone
you like – but only two'?

That magical light is starting to fade now, Joel's running about tidying up stray bits of wood and a few tools.

I stand at the kitchen window and grab my little black
book from my nearby rucksack. There's a blotch of
Yorkie smeared across one corner and the whole thing is
looking tattier than before this adventure began. I tear it

open and race through to Mark chapter 9. Another scene of awesome light and drama. What's Jesus just been up to then – before this epic close encounter happens?

Oh. That makes sense. That's why he needs time out, that's why he needs to compare notes with the prophets of old, men who had to battle with the world and do miracles and wonders to make the folk sit up and take notice.

He's just broken the news to the lads for the first time about his impending doom.

'I'm gonna die, boys, it's the way it's gonna be.'

Breaking that news, stating it aloud, cannot have been easy. Must have ripped into him like a chainsaw through firewood. It's one thing to hear that in your mind, quite another to speak it out and give it legs. Once it's out there it's like a dangerous animal, sitting, waiting, prowling around him. Always there in the shadows. The promise of pain and death. I guess Jesus knows what it's like to have to break bad news to people, he knows what it is to have to talk about losing what you love.

That's why his lionheart Father musters this meeting. He knows his boy's limping right now. He needs a bit of perspective. Some team time, some R&R. He needs to meet other guys who've lived through the fury and frustrations that come with following God. Get up that mountain, Jay – get up there and get powered up again. I wonder what they chatted about?

'Moses, Eli, you have no idea what it's like down here.'

'Oh yea we do! We've been there, thanks very much.'

'Nightmare, isn't it?'

And in the background Peter and the lads watch, their mouths torn open like hollow craters, lips flapping like fish, Peter thinking this is the end of everything.

'Jesus,' he yells, 'this is amazing. Let's stay up here forever. This is a perfect end to the story. I told you you

were the Christ, the One. See, I was right. This is fantastic, let's not bother with that other stuff down there.
Let's put up a couple of designer tents, top of the range,
and just move in.'

And Jesus chucks out light for a while, unmasks himself and comes out of the closet; and God can't hold back
and has to join in.

'That's my boy. You can do it.'

Eventually the fireworks fade and the party's over.
And Jesus takes his mates back down to reality. But he's
focused again – more than that – he's on fire. Then he's
met by real life and a bunch of people who can't muster
a fistful of faith to heal a possessed child. And he's up
and at 'em. Inspired, frustrated.

'Oh! For goodness sake! Can't you get it? You people
drive me up the wall!'

He's just been up there with two guys who don't need
to have faith. Moses and Elijah understand, they're on
the same page as Jesus. These people don't even have
the right book. How long must he put up with them?

Real life hits him like a train and – like us after a holiday or time out – he has to do some adjusting. The disciples are gagging to stay up on mount happy: why go
back to reality? The leaky roof, the bills, the noisy neighbours, the dullness of every day. But Jesus is adamant.

Sorry lads, we're going to get more involved with life,
not less.

The light's rapidly running away from Joel's garden
now. Joel comes in and we start throwing bits of food
about. We discuss what glorious culinary masterpiece
we're gonna make. Then we pick up the phone and dial
in some beers and pizza instead.

Joel chucks a few logs on the fire and as the dying sun
turns the fading blue sky to a muddy red, we settle
down with the drinks and food and watch *About a Boy*

followed by *Withnail and I* – two movies that I find profoundly heartwarming, funny and inspiring.

I find myself wondering whether that's much of the problem with the dull nature of church for us blokes. The kind of stories, characters and symbols that would energise us guys are rarely used. My life was once saved by the wayward writings of men who weren't afraid to laugh out loud about the madness of being male. Don't do much laughing about that in church. Yet I seem to recall another real man expounding the power of truth – it'll set you free, he told the men who followed him. If only we dare indulge ourselves occasionally.

18. Jeremiah's Pants

Jeremiah 1:1–12; 13:1–11; 3:1–5; 18; 19:1–3

Jeremiah's depressed. He's lying on his bed and he doesn't want to get up today. He can't see much reason to do anything any more. Life stinks. He's thinking about the book of Job, mumbling the bitter words his father showed him recently.

'Cursed be the day of my birth, and cursed be the night when I was conceived. Let that day be turned to darkness. Let it be lost even to God on high, and let it be shrouded in darkness. Yes, let the darkness and utter gloom claim it for its own. Let a black cloud overshadow it, and let the darkness terrify it. Let that night be blotted off the calendar, never again to be counted among the days of the year, never again to appear among the months. Why didn't I die at birth as I came from the womb? Why did my mother let me live? Why did she nurse me at her breasts? For if I had died at birth, I would be at peace now, asleep and at rest. Why was I not buried like a stillborn child, like a baby who never lives to see the light?'

Why is he alive? What's the point? He's a fearful teenager: life seems dark and dreary to him so much of the time. Black clouds frequently overshadow him, darkness frequently terrifies him; storm clouds grip his mind and he can't shake them off. He imagines all kinds of wild things. Is he mad?

And as he lies there staring at the ceiling, the roof evaporates in front of his eyes and the bright blue sky breaks through. The sun's piercing out there, which is odd because when he looked out of the window, it was raining and gloomy. Oh, it's not the sun blazing up there, it's a man's face, a figure is peering down at him through the roof, now it's clambering down. There's a thud as the glowing body lands beside his bed. It reaches down and the burning fingers touch his lips, then the Man whispers something.

'I know you, Jeremiah, I knew you before you were born. And I know it was a difficult birth. I wired you up in your mother's womb and before you ever saw the light of day, I had plans for you. Before you burst out and began kicking and screaming, I had already chosen you. You have the gift of communication, Jeremiah, and if you use it, you can be my mouthpiece to the world.'

That would have made some young men yell for joy. Not Jeremiah.

'Lord,' he mutters, 'I can't speak for you! I'm way too young! No one will ever listen.'

'Don't say that,' the Man replies, 'never say that, don't let anyone look down on you because you're young. Forget that, instead remember this, I want you to go wherever I send you and say whatever I tell you. I will give you thoughts and pictures and ideas, I've already been doing it. Don't be afraid of the people, don't worry what they'll think, for I will be with you and I'll take care of you. D'you hear me? D'you realise who is speaking to you? This is not just anyone. This is the one who made you.'

Jeremiah nods, but he's too fazed to do more. The Man claps a hand across his mouth and for a moment Jeremiah tastes honey on his lips.

'My words, Jeremiah, are in your mouth now. Be faithful to them. Honour them. The words of life and death, don't devalue them. Ever. And don't argue. Look, what's that?'

The Man points towards the window – Jeremiah sees an almond tree. It's a little ragged and dripping with rainwater but it's out there.

'Remember that. You'll see them everywhere; let it be a reminder – I'm always watching, always present with you. When you see one, you'll know I keep my promises. Life and death, Jeremiah, life and death. Now get up, get dressed and stop messing about. You have plenty to say and plenty to do.'

That was thirty years ago but it seems like yesterday. It always seems like yesterday, that vision of God. Jeremiah's been seeing almond branches ever since. And plenty more besides. He's tried to be faithful, and it's not easy when you're a miserable goat with a chip on your shoulder and have so many days of darkness. But he hangs on and he tries his best and those almond branches keep bringing him back to what matters.

And that's why he's burying his underwear.* He bought these pants a while back. Good quality, trendy, nice linen. Now he's shoving them into the filthy ground, burying them in the dirt between the rocks. They'll certainly rot. He'll never wear them again. By the time he digs them up, they'll be decayed and covered in mildew. He just hopes that God won't command him to put them back on. He has a hunch that this is about the state of the nation. That was once clean, new, bright. Not any more. The people's stupidity and pride have made everything rotten. It's all falling apart. Just like his pants.

---

* The Amplified Bible, King James Bible and Contemporary English Version describe it as a loincloth, although the NIV translates it as a belt. It is also described as a loincloth in the Lion Handbook, and The Message Bible says shorts.

I have a mild form of Obsessive Compulsive Disorder. OCD you call it when you're in a hurry.

This really doesn't help with the matter of selecting your underwear.

There are times when I'm literally paralysed by choice. I stare at my sock drawer and wonder which pair is *the right pair* for today. There must be a *right pair*. Getting dressed is like choosing the Holy Grail in that Indiana Jones movie. Choose well and you will live. Choose badly and the end might come. Which socks are divinely appointed? Which pair has the potential to change the world and alternately which pair would be cataclysmic if I chose them?

I know it all sounds madness as I lay it down here. But I get my emotions tied up with perfectly logical decisions and then the fear comes on me and I must get it right.

It's the same in Cutter's. If my favourite chair by the fire has been unlawfully occupied by someone else's fat backside, then which other seat should I take? I need to get it right.

And it's not only about choice. Have I really shut the fridge door? Have I really switched off the tap? Have I really locked the car? So many things to check, so many times to check them. I glance out of the window now and see my Money-pit parked up in Joel's drive. I've been so preoccupied I'd forgotten to worry about it till now.

Throwing things away is tough too – mustn't throw something away that's important, mustn't get that wrong. Must check every empty bag, every discarded package. Washing hands is a tough one and a problem very common to OCD sufferers. We don't want to contaminate things. We must be clean. It can all mean that life takes an awfully long time.

Even as I write this book I have difficulties – the right word, the right comma in the right place. Sounds bonkers, but trust me – many of us live with the daily trauma of these things.

There are of course many times when I throw caution to the wind and just leap in with both feet. The world might end but what the hell. I'll volunteer anyway; I'll make that choice whatever. I'll choose that way even if it means the sky falls on my head and the four horsemen come knocking on my door with a death warrant.

And talking of both feet brings me nicely back to my socks. It's the next morning and the sun's streaming into my room through a fracture in the curtains. I'm sitting on the bed staring into my rucksack – I didn't bother unpacking, I'm a bloke let loose on my own, for goodness sake. We got to bed really late after going out to catch a late night showing of the latest Bond movie. Then on the way back we nipped into Burger King to get way too many cheeseburgers for our own good with extra big chocolate and lard milk shakes on the side. So I've had too much fat and too little sleep, and choosing socks always puts me under duress. Eventually I shut my eyes and grab a pair, any pair, and hurriedly shove them on. I doubt if Jeremiah had OCD or whatever the Judaic equivalent was. Was it a nightmare for him deciding which pair of pants to bury? I doubt it. He seems a fairly depressive type though, and had plenty of bad news to bring to people.

> 'Jeremiah, just go over and sit by that prostitute. Go on. When people stop and ask you why you're sat there touting for business, tell them that's exactly what they're doing. Out and about offering themselves to anyone who'll have them. Go on, don't be shy.'
>
> 'Jeremiah, stop that cooking: get down to the pottery shop and see how they make those pots you're using. Go

on, you'll see a bloke get it wrong and crush the clay so he can start again. That's what the people need. Reshaping, remoulding, reworking. They haven't come out the way I thought they would. They're wonky jars, Jeremiah, dysfunctional tubs. But I'm always ready to reboot and start again. Whenever they stop and do a U-turn, I'll be right there turning with them. It's as easy and as difficult as that. Now buy one of those jars, no, not a little one, get the biggest and the best. That's it. Beautiful isn't it? Now take it out into the valley and smash it up. I want it in a million pieces. But don't do it alone, throw a party, get all the priests and leaders out there. Make sure they see that what is magnificent can be trashed forever.'

And in the end he upset so many people, he ended up like dreamer Joe – down a whacking great well. Sitting in the dark fearing for his life. Like so many saints since.

But they lifted him out of the depths – and shoved him in some stocks. Then they freed him and handed him the death sentence. And in between all the rough stuff he kept on and on, he just wouldn't shut up. Figs, fires and fruitcake all featured in his prophetic doings. He even dressed up like an ox once.

And I do love the story about his underwear. God'll use anything, won't he? He just can't stop himself from getting involved with us. He won't hold himself back. He made us so he could talk to us, so why wouldn't he keep calling us up, speed dialling planet Earth? Seems to me he crops up all over the place. Even in your sock drawer.

And God reveals he can do cheesy humour too. Maybe Jeremiah liked pantomime jokes, maybe he bought the *Sun* and guffawed at its terrible headlines. Maybe he'd heard his vicar father crack so many sermon jokes he was used to it. Either way, God's straight in there with a quick pun. My little black book tells me so anyway. Apparently the word for almond branch here is the same as the word for watching.

So I suppose nowadays God would have grabbed Jerry by the shoulder, turned his head towards the nearest timepiece and said, 'Remember I'm clocking you, Jeremiah: whenever you see one of those and hear the ticking, think of that. Whenever you look at that thing on your wrist remember, I'm watching.'

> And now he has a piece of 'Carry On' humour for Jeremiah.
>
> 'Bury your boxers mate. Lay your longjohns to rest. Shovel your shorts. Plant your pants.'
>
> What? Jeremiah hangs his head and wonders. Is it just a mad hunch or is that really another shove from the Man?

Sometimes it seems that God spends his whole time looking for friends who will make themselves look stupid, people who'll do what he has done so many times – humiliate themselves to cross the great divide – jam a stick in the spokes of society to stop the wheels of madness grinding us further and further into unholy nothingness.

> 'Why Lord? Why have I got to do this stupid thing?'
>
> 'Because I need something so ordinary, so regular, a symbol that will remind people on a daily basis about what really matters. Something that will wake them up to reality every morning. They've all got underwear, they all put it on. Well, most of 'em, anyway. Every time they fish out their frillies and wash out their Y-fronts, every time they jiggle their jockstraps and clean their kecks, every time they turn their briefs inside out so they

can re-use them – I want them to remember your pants. I want them to see and remember what happened when you buried them – how useless and weak and pathetic they looked when you dug them up and paraded them around town. Yes I'm afraid so, Jeremiah, soon I want you to go back, dig 'em up again and then wear them out and about to show people what becomes of the things that get neglected and buried. I want something effective, something graphic. It may seem stupid, but believe me they'll never forget it.'

Poor old Jeremiah.

The next time you put on your underwear, spare a thought for him.

19. Men on Fire

1 Kings 19:1–18; Matthew 11:2–10; Malachi 4:5

Elijah and John are both big men. Outdoors kind of guys. Both wear wild clothes and roughly hacked beards. They have foghorn voices and command an awful lot of attention. They worry very little about what people think of them, they don't sleep much and aren't known for their culinary expertise. One day they'll be mistaken for one and the same guy.

But not yet. Right now Elijah's on the run. He thought revival was coming, he thought life was gonna be one long Song of Songs from here on. But look at him, legging it halfway across the desert, breathless even though he's fighting fit, all dressed down and nowhere to go. Eventually he can go no more, collapses under a tree and begs to die.

'This job's too hard. Take me God, I've had enough.'

'What you doing here, Elijah?'

Elijah sits up. He must have dozed off. There's a strange warm smell in the air and a Man standing right next to him.

'Where did you come from?'

'None of your business. Get up, Elijah, get up and get some food down you, you're starving.'

'What?'

The Man points to a nearby rock.

So that's the smell. Freshly baked bread. And a cool flask of water.

'How d'you manage that out here in the desert?'

'None of your business. You ask too many questions, Elijah. If I told you, I'd have to kill you. Now eat.'

And the Man turns and walks away into the sun, but long before he would have been out of sight, he's disappeared.

Elijah doesn't take orders from anyone but there's something about this Man. So he eats, drinks and lies down again.

'Wake up!'

Elijah stirs and stares up into the hot sun. The Man's back.

'I thought I told you to eat?'

'I did eat.'

'All of it! You got a long way to go. Don't make me come back a third time. You won't like me if I come back a third time.'

'Don't like you now . . .'

Elijah mutters to himself as the man does his disappearing act again. He scoops up the rest of the bread, shoves it into his mouth with his blackened fingers then pours the water down his throat. He sleeps again, then as the sun fades, he starts to travel. The food and rest have cleared his mind, he sees where he is and realises where he's going. Moses' mountain, the mountain of God, maybe there'll be some inspiration for him there. If nothing else, with his belly full, he no longer feels like dying.

Forty days later, still alive and extremely tanned, he crawls into a cave in the mountain. Whatever happens now, it's up to God. Kill or cure, something's gotta happen.

'Elijah, what are you doing here?'

'Waiting for you. The angel told me to come. Where are you, Lord?'

There's the sound of a divine sigh, not unlike the one Moses heard in the shadow of that same mountain all those years ago.

'Elijah, come outside.'

The moment he steps foot out of the cave, the hurricane hits him. Elijah's body is picked up like a bit of litter and smashed against the side of the mountain. Rocks break loose above him and come crashing past him, one of the smaller ones leaving a gash in his shoulder.

'Is that you, Lord? Are you here?'

'Nope, keep watching.'

The rumbling begins gently, but it soon throbs to an ear-shredding roar, as if the lion of Judah has been prematurely woken from a good lie-in. The ground shakes and bends and bits of it break up in front of him. Smoke and lava belch upwards between the cracks. Gargantuan sparks fly up and ignite nearby trees. The wind joins in and whips the flames into a storming furnace, sucking plants and tumbleweed into this flaming twister. Elijah has to leap and spin to avoid being toasted alive.

'Is that you? Where are you?'

The earthquake crashes into silence. The fiery tornado swallows itself. The winds begin to die too and suddenly there's a deathly hush about the mountain. Elijah shivers, his bones feeling suddenly like ice.

'Lord? Where are you?'

He has to strain to hear the whisper.

'You thought it was about power, didn't you?' the little voice says. 'You thought you could pummel them into changing.'

'I've served you faithfully and where's it got me? Nowhere. I'm the only one left in this land who cares about you. Everyone else is dead and I will soon be too. What else can I do? If they won't repent after that showdown with the Baal prophets, nothing'll make them change.'

'You're misled, Elijah, it's not about power. That won't win people. It's about relationship. And you're wrong, you're not alone. There are hundreds of others out there who know me well. I can kick up a storm anytime I like, Elijah, I can just snap my fingers and it's done. But I can't make anyone follow me. I have all the power in the universe – I don't have all the relationships. Go back, Elijah, start again. Here's a list of jobs to keep you busy and out of trouble for a while. And you see that name at the top of the list. That's your successor. If you think it's over, then maybe it is coming to an end for you. Elijah, anoint that guy and then we'll talk again.'

John's depressed too, but he's not on the run. He's in prison under sentence of death. He can't go chasing storms and hiding in caves. He'll never see Moses' mountain or the desert again.

'John, what can we do for you?'

He looks out through the bars at his two visitors, old friends who've stuck with him through thick and thin.

'I'm confused,' he says. 'Remember my cousin?'

They nod. They can hardly forget, he's everywhere now.

'He's big news, John. You were right, he got bigger and you got smaller.'

John winces: his followers talk straighter than he does.

'That's what bothers me. I hear he spends a lot of time telling stories, chatting to women and picking up kids.'

They nod.

'Why doesn't he confront the Pharisees, why isn't he turning the nation around?'

'He does confront them, they argue all the time.'

'Argue! That doesn't get anything done. Talk talk talk. No better than the priests and politicians. I didn't picture a Messiah like this! I had a vision of a man who would separate the good from the bad. A warrior who could wipe out the corruption and unmask the liars. This nation needs a good clean-out. A good pruning. It needs hacking back to the roots. Where's his axe? Where's his fighting spirit? You can't change the world by stroking kids and sweet-talking women!'

'What should we do?'

'Go and find the truth! Confront him! Is he the Messiah or not? And bring back the facts while I'm still breathing.'

Jesus dusts his hands and laughs. He laughs a lot these days. Watching the blind see and the disabled dance has to put a smile on your lips. A little girl blind from birth is running around grabbing people by the ears and measuring the size of their noses. He sits on a rock and picks the damp sand and spit from under his nails.

'Jesus!'

Another cry for help. He's still grinning as he looks up and sees the men coming.

'D'you have a sick relative?' he asks.

'No, we have a frustrated friend.'

Jesus frowns, the people nearby fall silent. The men's tone is abrupt, aggressive.

'Your cousin sent us.'

Jesus' face lights up again.

'John? John! How is he? Does he have food? It's so long since I saw him. We had such great times as kids, he was always dragging me out on some wild adventure. He'd come over with Aunt Liz and . . .'

'Never mind about that, that's irrelevant. Are you the Messiah?'

'What?'

'Are you the Messiah?'

'But tell me about John.'

'There's nothing to tell. He just wants to know the truth. Should he be looking for someone else? Did he get it wrong?'

Jesus shakes his head. This is what it's going to be like now. Conflict and anger, it'll follow him wherever he goes, all down the ages.

The little girl dances by, humming to herself. Jesus smiles again and beckons to her. He stands her in front of him and places his hands on her shoulders.

'This is what John was talking about,' one of the men mutters out of the side of his mouth to the other, 'kids and women.'

'Yes!' Jesus yells and they jump.

'The blind see, the lame walk, lepers are cured, the deaf hear, the dead are raised to life. It's not a dull life out here. The bent reeds are not broken off. Tell John the kingdom of heaven is rife in the streets. And tell him . . . tell him that though I offend some people – many people – there are lots of happy people who are not offended by me.'

'What does that mean?'

'John has a quick brain – he'll work it out.'

After that brief hiatus with my underwear I chuck on yesterday's clothes and venture downstairs.

Joel's in the kitchen cooking up a storm, eggs, pancakes, bacon and hash browns. I tell him how good it is to be here. He nods and brews up some coffee.

I wander into the dining room and gaze across the lawn at a tiny deer-like creature busy bounding across the grass.

'What's that?' I yell, pointing, even though Joel's out of eye shot.

'A muntjac!' he yells back, 'A sort of cross between a deer and a rabbit. A raving mutant if you like. An X-man of the venison variety. Sweet little creatures. See 'em from time to time.'

'So is there a chief X-Muntjac in a steel wheelchair with shiny crosses on it?'

'Yea, and the other normal animals have a military wing to try and wipe them out. They're called stoats. And talking of slaughtered animals – your bacon's ready. Come on, eat up and I'll take you to the gun club. Mike's bringing his .308. He'll be here soon.'

Mike-the-Bike is Joel's local best friend, i.e. a best friend who actually operates like a best friend, instead of me who appears less often than a sunny bank holiday. He arrives on a massive BMW motorbike and lurches into an account of a night spent losing at poker.

He has a bushy beard, leather trousers and a shaved head. I think he used to be in ZZ Top. Or maybe he thinks he used to be in ZZ Top. I expect him to break into *Viva Las Vegas* any minute.

I know I'm supposed to love everyone but I just find him intimidating. He's my Goliath – by which I don't mean I'm gonna deck him with a pebble, of course. Unlike Joel I just struggle to be natural in his presence, I end up sticking out my chin, adopting a cockney accent and flexing my shoulders every three minutes. I turn into a cross between Del Boy Trotter and Bruce Forsyth.

It's funny – he and Mike have a lot in common – bikes, poker, guns – yet I feel a world apart from Mike, and a soul mate to Joel. In Mike's presence I feel smaller, in Joel's I feel bigger. I just don't have any reference points in Mike's world. He comes from planet swagger. My small Christian worldview must seem like baloney to someone like him. Like I'm Shaggy in *Scooby Doo* and no one's told me the mystery of life is really just a bloke in a rubber mask. I'm just one of those pesky kids who pops up in a new technicolour episode once a week pretending life is one big spooky adventure; whereas Mike inhabits a man's world where people really do drink fifteen pints, chew tobacco, strip down their Harleys and indulge in pool, soccer, arm-wrestling, darts, dominoes and sky-diving on a regular basis. As I stand here looking at him now, all those logical sensible reasons I've discovered for having faith turn to pork scratchings in my head. Why don't I wear an earring and have a bull neck the size of his? When did I enrol in the Frank Spencer school of life? I look at Mike and Joel laughing and wonder what I'm doing here. Why does Joel put up with this incompetent whiny stream of camel spit that passes for me? Somehow he happily straddles the continents of Mike and Me (and if we're following this analogy through then Mike's probably North America and I'm some lump of rock off the Falklands that even the penguins don't want); somehow he keeps a foot on both islands. I know I'll never manage that. I just don't have the inside leg measurement.

I guess it's the faith that keeps Joel and me on the same land mass. Joel doesn't go to church, hasn't bothered in years. But he's always talking about God and he's a better evangelist than me by miles. He's also refreshingly straightforward. I can be myself with him, expose the dark side of my force and allow my toxic waste to leak out. He doesn't pretend. I can talk about anything and joke about everything – sex, religion, politics, pet hates (i.e. political correctness, I.D. cards and London), and oh yeah, those embarrassing medical conditions that creep up on you as you reach middle-age.

Mates like that are rare.

Apart from knowing each other forever we've seen each other through so much, good times and bad, thick and wise, puberty and manhood. Okay, so most of the time we were half a country apart, but thank God for phones, eh? So many seasons came and went.

Singleness, schooling, unemployment, marriage: divorce in his case, dadhood in mine. Fire, fury, faith, doubt, debt and dating – we've seen each other through it all. As Joel once said, 'There's only incontinence and decomposing to look forward to now.'

Joel makes a good-natured joke about my running away and wanting to prove myself.

Mike looks over to me and offers his bike.

'This is what you need,' he says, 'something big between your legs.'

I laugh too loudly and look for the nearest hole in the ground. There isn't one.

'Seriously, mate, d'you wanna give it a go?'

He is serious. He's offering me his bike.

I flex my shoulders, stick out my chin and saunter over.

'Try sitting on it,' he says.

He lets me take the handlebars and I swing my leg smoothly over the saddle. Except I don't. I don't swing high enough and catch my foot on the rear tyre. I stagger and try again. Oh dear. Third time lucky? Yes! I'm on. It feels good, it feels manly, it feels . . . bloomin' heavy. It's going, it's going over. It's about to crush my left leg.

'Easy!'

Mike and Joel wade in and rescue me from the terrors of a stationary motorbike. I get off it a lot quicker than I got on.

'It's er . . . big isn't it?' I mutter sheepishly, backing away from it as if it's a rabid animal.

'You'll get used to it. It's easier once it's going.'

Mike's genuinely a whole lot nicer about this than I deserve. In fact he's probably a whole lot nicer than I am. I just feel an idiot. Another disastrous attempt to prove my manhood goes wildly out of sync. Will I never turn into Arnold Shterminator?

Joel slips inside to make a brew. Mike goes with him but I stay outside, surreptitiously rubbing the bruise on my thigh. It hurts but not as much as the shiner on my dignity. When this kind of thing happens I'm just a little kid again, standing around on the touchline not being picked for the football team. I was too studious, too bookish, too boring to score goals or make runs. I did score a try once when I found myself on a team that couldn't care less about rugby. The ball came my way, I picked it up and ran. Fortunately in the right direction. It's the zenith of my sporting achievements. I can still recall to this day hearing the urgent cry of 'Put it down between the posts!' I probably didn't. But for a moment there I wasn't me, I was – whoever was big in rugby at the time.

Staring at Joel's pitch-sized garden brings it all back. It wasn't exactly the winning try at Twickenham but for a few brief seconds it felt like I could actually play some sport.

> 'Look, I am sending you the prophet Elijah before the great and dreadful day of the Lord arrives. His preaching will turn the hearts of parents to their children, and the hearts of children to their parents. Otherwise I will come and strike the land with a curse.'

Elijah and John are men like Mike and Joel. They say it straight. They don't mess about. They don't suffer fools. Thankfully not every hero in the good book is cut from that cowhide – but some are. And how we need 'em. They scare the pants off me and I'd probably make my excuses and slip out the back door if I bumped into them today. But they were strong men taking hold of the faith. With all their obvious chinks too. Elijah was so stubborn, he couldn't see a piece of good advice when it slapped him round the ear and jabbed him in the eye.

'Eat, Elijah, you're hungry.'

Wow! Seems God's practically minded. Elijah may be a giant of the faith, but he still needs fast food and a lie-in every so often. John may have blazed a trail through a snake-strewn wilderness, but he needed reassurance when he found himself alone and out of the spotlight. We all need sound advice and reassurance, and I thank God for Joel. Food, sleep, encouragement and a good ear to bend. You can't beat it.

20. No More Heroes

2 Timothy 3:15–17

Dear Timothy, (and every other bloke on the planet)

Now listen up. Listen! You guys have the Bible and some of you have been taught about it since you were lads, and digging into it has given you the guidance to receive the kind of future that only comes by trusting in Jesus Christ. All of the Bible is inspired by God and is useful to teach us what is true and to make us realise what is wrong in our lives. All of it. But many of you guys haven't got a clue what's in there. You pussyfoot about on the fringes of the New Testament and never set foot in the Old. A couple of verses here, a stray bit of Gospel there. Believe me, I know it's hard work, I wrote a lot of it – but it's worth chewing on. Get an intelligent faith, don't leave your brain in the bathroom when you meet together. Use it. Ask, seek, knock and look deeper. Don't take it all at face value.

Serve God with all your mind. Everyone in the Bible was a real person once – those pages are full of people like you struggling each day to follow God. They didn't live in days when the skies were writ large with divine encouragement and guidance. They were just like us – they struggled to keep going. They had days of sulking and rebelling and doubting and disbelieving. Read between the lines. Jeremiah, Job, Elijah and David all had days when they wished they were dead. Dig deeper and you'll see yourself in these guys. It'll hearten you and teach you so much more of what it means to follow God. This handbook is God's way of preparing us and fully equipping us for every good thing that he wants us to do. And he has a truckload of stuff for us to get involved with. So don't hold back. Find what you can do and do it. There's more to this book than the Prodigal Son and a few verses about love. Study the heroes, learn from their mistakes and madness, from their faith and failures. Gain from their experience. How did they pray? How did they think? How did they react? How did they change their little bit of the planet? And take careful note – God called them according to the way he'd wired them up, according to the kind of lives they'd lived and background they had. David didn't model himself on Moses and Moses didn't attempt to ape Abraham. Stop these stories every so often, freeze the action and ask yourself, what can I learn right now? Take note of all the voices in the Bible – not just mine. The prophets, the kings, the artists, the writers. Don't view the Bible through my small lens – view it through the eyes of Jesus.

Later, Paul.

You can just imagine the spin an ad agency would apply to keep a reality block on the good book.

Right, so you've come to us with this . . . what d'you call it? Bible? Hmm, the name'll never catch on. So let's start with this old guy Abraham – cool father of faith. Founder of . . . everything. Great big beard, great big staff, great big liar . . . what? Liar? Put his life on the line? That's good, isn't it? Oh – put his wife on the line – that's not so good. Can we just not mention that bit? Keep it quiet . . . He did it twice? Keep it quiet twice then.

Samson? Great! Tough guy. Warrior. Brave man. Lots of nice hair. We like him. Angel announces his birth, he's full of the spirit, great holy man. Used a lot of shampoo and conditioning products. Let's get a Samson range going then – Samsonsilk. He what? He killed lots of men and bedded lots of women. Er hmm, let's not confuse people, let's just cut to that bit at the end when he brought the house down.

David – king – party animal – rock'n'roll man – general – hero – poet – catapult kid – twang! Great shot! No giants any more. What? Bad father? Bad husband? Moody old . . . Can we just not mention that? Let's say: worship leader, songster, man after God's heart and peeping To . . . No! No peeping bits.

Jesus – great! Son of God, saved the world, healed everyone, told some ripping yarns . . . What? He had a crisis of faith? In the middle of the night? Didn't always know what was happening next? Wasn't always in control? He didn't want to die for the sins of the world? He hung around with prostitutes and lowlife? That's no good. We can't have any of that. Hang on, no, it'll be all right, we tell everyone they were nice prostitutes and friendly sinners – didn't actually do any sex or crime or anything. The girls just looked a bit tarty – in a conservative, attractive sort of way. The crooks were loveable rogues. Like Fagin or the Artful Dodger.

Prodigal Son? Now that'll sell a million. We like that one – great story. Perfect. Son comes home, hugs dad, happy sunset. Dead cow. The end. What? Older brother's in the bedroom packing his bags, he's been out there cussing and ruining the last scene? Well, let's re-cut that. Older son hugs brother, tears run down their cheeks. A dozen children join them, all beautiful obviously. They break into song – something from *Annie*. Nobody argues, no one's unhappy. We could call it the alternative ending. The director's cut.

Have we got any women in there? It doesn't matter so much now but in a few years' time, they'll be getting all huffy about the women thing . . . Rahab? Cool name. What – rescued spies – perfect! An action woman. Lara Croft. Great. She was courageous. Bold. Sassy. She was what? A hooker? A reformed hooker you mean? No, just a hooker. Not one of the ones Jesus knocked around with surely . . . Let's just say she was a good businesswoman, we don't have to say what her business was.

Paul – great! Started the church, converted loads of people, preached a lot, wrote funky letters, be good, don't be bad; get it right, don't get it wrong; wear hats, don't wear hats . . . what? He said he was what? The worst sinner ever? Really? What – worse than Bin Laden? He was what? Bit of a control freak, didn't condemn slavery . . . Let's have a look . . . Can we just cut him out of the New Testament? He was the New Testament. Oh.

Hang on.

It'll be okay cos I know these Christians: they'll just read the surface stuff – they won't go too deep – we'll get away with it. They'll just read the words, they won't read the people's lives. It'll be cool. We'll just keep throwing in that stuff about being nice and loving everybody. Maybe Paul could have a big droopy-eyed Basset hound, or a Labrador puppy that keeps running off with his letter to the Romans . . .'

We spend an hour or two at the firing range – it's on a farm buried deep in the heart of nowhere. I instantly like the atmosphere and the friendly banter. Lots of guys with their gun collections, tea, sandwiches, combat jackets and earphones. Lots of unzipping of gun cases and talk about the size of one's cartridges. Everyone's blasting at targets and swapping stories about the price of black powder and the latest gun laws. As far as I can tell no one is there training to shoot up the nearest shopping mall. They all seem as harmless as a box of blanks. Joel reckons it's as friendly as any church he's known.

Mike cracks off a few dozen shots with some hefty fifty calibre firestick that has a kick like Jonny Wilkinson while Joel keeps apace with him nearby with his Winchester. I step in every so often and show them what happens when you neglect to put a bullet in the chamber or shoot straight. Joel's Winchester has a pleasing action, the empty cartridges fly out of the chamber when you cock it, just like in all the best cowboy films. Perfect. I just have to remember to duck every so often so I don't get one in the eye.

I try not to be too nosy but I can't help watching these guys and wondering how messy their lives are. No worse than mine, I'm sure. A small part of me, a very small part, would love to haul out my Bible and somehow help these guys see they are right here in these pages. This is a book about the people, for the people: blokes and boys, old fellas and young guns. But the problem is, it's now seen as such a religious book. They'd never think of it as being about life – and especially not their life. What's the Bible got to say to a group of guys who meet together of an afternoon to joke, learn, sup tea, swap stories and fire off a few rounds? Surely the guys in the Bible are nothing like that. Aren't they?

This book's had such bad press. And I guess some of these guys aren't big readers anyway. So that's the other problem – everything in the good book was originally lived out, not read out. And names like Othniel, Methuselah and Nebuchadnezzar were names you could encounter down the local gun club. They weren't old-fashioned and weird; they were normal and relevant. It all seems to conspire to put a wedge between the good guys and the good book. It's so blaggin' frustrating.

I sigh and shake my head. Joel hands me a box of cartridges.

'You all right there?' he asks.

I nod, load up and take out my frustration on a cardboard target.

21. Licence to Kill

Esther 9:1–17

It's March 7th. As day dawns over Susa, the sound of axes being sharpened rings through the city. Swords are being honed and knives likewise. The Jews have long feared the coming of this day – the day of punishment, the day of annihilation. Their enemies have long been preparing to rise up and slaughter them. The king's decreed it. It's totally legal. But at the last moment there's a reprieve. Another decree goes out and it isn't Persian weapons being prepared – it's Jewish. The hunter has become the hunted. The killing begins when a band of young men arrives at the house of a local official. They exchange angry words, the household gather at the door to see what the trouble is. The men outside force their way in and, with axes and spears, they murder and mutilate the entire family. Grandparents and children included.

Crowds of Jews begin to gather in all the cities. They're jubilant. They thought they were going to die today but it seems they're gonna kill. Long-held grudges quickly bubble to the surface and those folk they've long despised are dealt with first. Swift injustice. Take 'em out and hack 'em up. It's hard physical work, but they go at it with a vengeance. They're determined to settle old scores. This is their time: after years of skulking in the shadows as second-class citizens, they're now top dog. And they're going to make the most of it. The gutters run red and the refuse heaps pile up with bodies and bits of corpses.

That evening, after the first day of the genocide, the king hears reports about the number of killings in the fortress of Susa.

He calls for his wife Esther. 'Your people have killed five hundred people in the fortress alone. Five hundred! This is madness. And that's just here, what do you think has been going on in the rest of the provinces?' The king is sweating. This is not what he expected when he gave the Jews free rein to defend themselves against an unjust law. This is anarchy, these people have lost all sense of purpose or conscience. 'Esther, what should I do? I made a grave mistake and I'm intent on correcting it. What more do you want? I promise it will be granted to you, I'm a man of my word. Just tell me and I'll do it. I want to make amends.'

Esther's face is impassive, giving away nothing. She's a mouthpiece for her uncle and she dare not make a mistake.

'If it please Your Majesty, give the Jews in Susa permission to do again tomorrow what they have done today, and have the bodies of Haman's sons hung from the gallows.'

The king beckons for more wine. He needs something to dull the horror. He drinks a goblet-full and nods.

'Whatever you want,' he says. 'Send out the servants, announce the glorious news. Let the people rejoice . . .'

So the king agrees, he's bound by his oath and the killing goes on.

Elsewhere the other Jews have gathered together to defend their lives and punish their enemies, and on 7th March alone they kill seventy-five thousand of their enemies, though they held back from doing any looting.

We pick up a DVD on the way back from the range. Interestingly enough it's called *Shooting Dogs* but has nothing to do with gun clubs or black powder. It's three o'clock by the time we get back and we settle down with a few beers to watch. I'm glad we didn't make popcorn. Suddenly we're plunged into a world of hatred and murder. Not the Agatha Christie kind of murder with a body in every library and an old woman with a brain the size of a sanitarium. This is far more sinister. This is the story of one of a thousand massacres during the hundred days of the Rwandan genocide back in 1994. The leaders of the majority Hutu tribe, fearing oppression from the minority Tutsis, incited their people to rise up and 'cut down the tall trees' as they called them. 'Kill the Tutsi cockroaches,' they announced frequently on local radio. And for one hundred days the Hutus did just that. They went from home to home and school to school, pulling out their enemies and butchering them. They set up road blocks to stop and search any who tried to leave. In a century of days they killed at least eight hundred thousand people. Eight thousand a day. Many Tutsis gathered in schools and colleges to hide from the slaughter, but they were often surrounded and murdered. *Shooting Dogs* is the story of one such incident.

Mike, not being an avid film fan, gave up a third of the way in and went outside to clean his guns. Joel spent the rest of the film in and out: ten minutes with me, ten minutes with Mike. I was absorbed in the movie and couldn't understand how anyone could treat the subject matter so lightly. Disturbed by the film and annoyed by the distractions, I end up with my head in a place of turmoil. It happens sometimes – you're just cruising along nicely when something jams a potato up your exhaust pipe. I end up storming out of the lounge during the final credits. It has little effect as Mike and Joel are in the kitchen laughing and playing poker. Poker is a perfect game for men. It involves bluff, risk and front and you can completely avoid looking stupid. If you don't want to show your meagre hand you just fold and throw in your cards. No one need ever know how pathetic your deal really is. I watch them play for a short time, inwardly fuming at their lack of respect, then I sigh loudly, throw them a strained look, grab my coat and make for the door. Mike waves at me.

'You don't wanna go out there, it's . . .'

I do go out there.

The weather's changed. There's a body-blasting wind and horizontal rain to go with it. I battle to make it down to the end of the drive and then out into the lane. There are houses to my left, fields to my right. I don't want anyone to see me out for a stroll in this weather looking stupid so I head for the fields. It's slow going but it suits my spirit at the moment. I'm torn about inside anyway, might as well get ripped to shreds on the outside too. The rain spatters my face and the wind continues to twist me right and left as I walk. The bruise on my leg from the BMW incident starts to throb again.

Why do people do that? Kill each other like that? How can they be so barbarous? How can they smile as they machete babies and smash skulls? The war party outside that school danced and chanted as they waited for the opportunity to go in for the kill. The signal was given with a referee's whistle. A whistle, the sound of sport and carnivals.

And why do people do that? Ignore someone else's story so they can drink beer and tell jokes. I feel the mother of all moods coming on me. This is decision point. I have a short time with Joel. I need to patch this up. He probably has no idea about my anger anyway, yet I still feel the need to clear the air. But I don't have it in me. Going back and facing the two of them is too hard. I keep walking, berating myself for my stupidity at coming here in the first place, choosing that movie, storming out and getting wound up by all this.

I don't have my Bible but I start thinking about Esther. Seventy-five thousand people got slaughtered in one day. One day! The Jews were given licence to defend themselves and it went horribly wrong. They took it as licence to kill. They were scared of being slaughtered so they drew first blood. And an awful lot of it there was too. Then they feasted and celebrated the death of their enemies.

God's had to live through so much, hasn't he? Our lives are shaken to the core, and rightly so, when we hear of another genocide, another massacre, another murder. God's had to live through every single one of them. There's nothing new under the sun and ever since Cain beat the life out of Abel, God's seen the worst that man can bring on man. It's a mad world all right. A very, very mad world.

People often ask how God can allow genocide. How can he sit back and watch such suffering from his fortress in heaven? But that's a very complicated question. Are we talking about the Rwandan genocide, or the Cambodian genocide, or the Jewish genocide? In Rwanda it was tribal, in Cambodia ideological, in Germany racial. This is a huge question and yet we expect a small answer. There is no easy reply because there is no easy question. It's like asking why $28.9512 \times 3.457 \times 4,9512 \times 57.951$ is such a difficult sum. It just is. The answer can't be simple because the puzzle is complicated. Human suffering is a complex problem involving hatred, selfishness, prejudice, self-preservation, accumulated fear, planetary weather fronts, climate, political power and fickle, insecure, impressionable people. And, to be honest, if we knew the answer to this, it would do very little for us. The staggering thing about Christian spirituality is that it dares believe in a God who curbs his power, makes himself small and visits every place of pain; suffering alongside the people who are frightened and dying. And that's a frustrating answer if you're chairing a televised debate.

Eventually, because it's dark and I'm fed up and my underpants are clinging to my bottom, I wander back. I arrive in the door with a bluster and my own personal rainstorm. Mike's gone and the kitchen's empty.

Joel hears me and comes in.

'Where've you been?'

'Oh, it was the movie: it got to me.'

'Didn't get to me.'

'I noticed.'

'What?'

I shake my head.

'I'm sorry, I just got uptight.'

'You could have told me what you were up to. You're soaking.'

We agree that I'll at least try and act my shoe size.

There's a kind of temporary cease-fire, although Joel's still a little bewildered. I shower, change and come down to find a couple of bowls of steaming chili and two doorstop sandwiches on the kitchen table.

'This'll put gas in your tank,' he says, 'literally.'

We eat hungrily and I mutter on about all those insignificant things that seem suddenly so significant when your guard's down. He tells me some of his current scares and problems and we end up chatting about sex. All roads lead there as far as men are concerned. We mutter on about that chestnut for quite a while. We eventually end up praying a chatty prayer for each other, using a hybrid language that's somewhere between Shakespearean English and cockney rhyming slang. Try as we might, we still end up putting on funny voices when we talk to God.

22. Jacob's Wrestling Match

Genesis 32:13–32

Jacob's had a great idea. He'll send his brother a huge mountain of presents – birthday, Christmas, Easter – all rolled into one. That'll soften him up. And not only that, he'll send all his gorgeous kids to meet the old barbarian ahead of him. Esau won't be able to kill his brother once he's set eyes on little Joe's angelic features. Jacob's children are good-looking. Esau won't butcher them. They are way too cute to slaughter. And in case that's not enough, he'll send the wives and lovers too. When Esau sees Rachel, his heart will melt. Women and children first, that'll do it. Esau may be coming with four hundred cussing blood-stained warriors but they'll surely not harm his family, they're not that bestial. By the time Jacob saunters into camp, Esau'll be putty in his hand. It's the perfect plan. He just has to sit it out by this campfire and wait for the dawn to rise. He just needs to stay awake and . . . He falls asleep.

A crunch of stones wakes him, there's the sound of a throat clearing and someone spits in the dirt.

Who's that? One of the kids come back looking for dad? Go back to your mother, we've got a long day ahead of us tomorrow. Another footfall, the scuffle of dead leaves. The sound of slowly exhaled breath. Jacob sits up. Maybe it's Esau. Maybe he's come ahead of time, knife in hand, retribution in his heart. Payback time.

Jacob's up in a flash.

'Who is it? Who's there?'

He sees a glint of metal as something shiny flashes in the firelight. Is it Esau? The man's big all right, all square shoulders and thick, thick muscles.

'Esau?'

The man says nothing.

'What do you want?'

Five seconds later he finds out. The man leaps over the fire and flattens Jacob. A fist smacks him across the chin and the stranger's body lands right on him, knocking him back into the dirt. They roll over and over, Jacob trying to break free. Somehow he does, scrambles up and starts to dust off his clothes. Mistake. Another fist smacks his nose and knocks his head backwards. He lurches, twists and collapses back onto the floor. A huge foot kicks at the dirt, showering his face with gritty sand and he flails about blindly. The man grabs him by the collar, picks him up and throws him at the fire. Jacob finally snaps. He feels the heat from the flames and recoils. He's still on the floor and now his clothes are on fire. He must get up, his eyes are burning but he forces them open. He beats out the flames on his robe with his bare hands. His palms blister but he keeps on. The man runs at him, and swings a foot at his head. At the last minute Jacob sees him, spins, swivels and leaps to his feet. The man misses his aim and loses his footing. Jacob's turn to kick sand in the face. The man staggers up and retreats. They stare at each other across the fire.

Jacob wipes the blood from his mouth and squints through the firelight at the dark figure.

'Who are you?' he hisses but there's no reply. Some heavy breathing but no reply.

Suddenly the stranger lunges at him again. Jacob sidesteps and grabs him round the neck. He holds him in a headlock but it won't last, he can feel the man fisting him in the back, close to his kidneys. Jacob releases the head and pulls away.

'What do you want? Money? I only have a little here . . . I sent it all away.'

'I know.'

The man speaks and his voice is massive. Like a roadful of motorbikes. He towers over Jacob like a granite statue.

'I don't want your money. I've come for you, Jacob. Two generations back, I promised your grandfather a family line that would stretch through time and on into forever. I won't let you deny me that.'

'What are you talking about?'

'I'm talking about you, Jacob. I want you to stop this ducking and diving. I can't fulfil the promise through Esau – it must be through you.'

The dark figure lunges at Jacob again and catches him off-guard. The stranger locks his arms around Jacob's waist and runs him backwards into a tree. Jacob beats on the man's back, the punches coming hard and fast until the man loosens his grip a little. Jacob squeezes free, twists aside, turns and kicks the man in the back of the knee. There's a cry of pain and the huge body doubles over. Now the odds are even. Now this shadowy figure will have a fight on his hands. He turns and they lunge at one another, grabbing forearms. The stranger is strong, more than equal to Jacob. They pull at each other, cough and spit with exertion. This is not Esau, Esau is a hairy guy. This man has the arms of God, the muscles of the Almighty. They fight on. Jacob does his best, pushes, pulls, throws his punches and levels his kicks. He takes what's coming, but doesn't flinch. They both end up bruised and bleeding. And as the sun comes up they stand at cross-purposes, both gasping, both clutching their chests, both hawking phlegm. This has been a night to remember. As the light dawns, Jacob realises the truth. Other men look on God and plead for mercy but Jacob has other things on his mind.

'Bless me . . . I won't let you go till you bless me . . .'

'If I bless you, you'll be weaker.'

'I can't get any weaker. What's my life worth? Nothing. My days are numbered. Bless me. Or kill me.'

'We met before, Jacob – d'you remember? That night at Bethel – angels and ladders. D'you remember?'

'Of course I remember. I promised I'd follow you.'

'*If* I blessed you. You're always after a blessing, Jacob. From your brother, from your father and now twice from me. Gimme, gimme, gimme. What about you giving, Jake? What about you putting your hand in your pocket?'

Jake's not so sure about that – so he shuts up and tries to fight the stranger again. But he can't win. He just can't cheat his way out of this one.

'Kill me, I'm tired of living. Don't let Esau do it.'

'Esau won't do it.'

'Why not?'

'Because he'll see an old man limping towards him and his heart will change. Now do you still want a blessing?'

Jacob nods. He's too tired to speak.

In the birth of a new day the stranger lays a calloused hand on Jacob's head. He speaks, then in a flash raises his other hand and smashes Jacob's hip. Jacob cries in pain and his body crumples. He'll limp forever now. But he'll never run from God again.

It's 1.45 in the morning and I can't sleep. I was just finally dozing off ten minutes back when a severe case of cramp slipped out of the darkness, crept up my left leg and hurled me from the bed. For a while I danced around like Mr Bean on speed, groaning and writhing and throwing myself on and off the furniture, willing the pain to go away. It felt like my leg was on fire. Eventually it all subsided and now I'm left like a limp rag and I can't straighten my calf properly. I'm also an awfully long way away from the land of nod. Totally in the wide-awake club now. I throw on two jumpers and a pair of jeans and gather myself together to make a huge mug of tea. I refuse to lie here tossing and turning and pretending I'm getting some rest. I venture downstairs. For a moment I wonder about the television – there's always the likelihood of something vaguely porno-graphic on TV at this time of night. But I fight off the urge to explore Channel Five and hurl myself towards the kettle. I check the water level, it's barely enough but I still jam the switch down anyway and gaze out of the window in time to catch a parade of phantom creatures bounding and tumbling across the lawn. Another munt-jac flies by, followed by a stoat zig-zagging across the grass in pursuit of a rabbit. Then there's a terrible shriek as the predator latches onto its prey. For a while horren-dous protracted screams ring out – macabre sounds, like fingers on a blackboard combined with the squeal and wrench of a door that hasn't been opened for thirty years. Death in the movies is never anything like real life, is it?

Thankfully, though not mercifully, the sound and the animal dies and the night falls silent again.

Then another rabbit appears, and another stoat, or maybe the same one keeping himself in mischief. More squealing and shrieking and killing. Fortunately it's all out of sight, beyond the waterhole in the bushes.

I flip back to Genesis. Enough barbarity. Let's get on to that heart-warming tale of Jacob and Esau, the twins who almost killed each other.

Against all the odds Abraham and Sarah have Isaac, laughing boy, you might call him. Only the laughter turns hollow when that inner compunction drives Abe to stretch out his boy on a chilly slab on a cold mountain. He lies there, eyes wide with terror and shock as his father unsheathes his knife, wipes dirt from the blade and raises it skyward. Abe smiles at his son, but his wet cheeks give him away. He waited a lifetime to be a father and now the dream's become a nightmare: not only must he lose his child, he has to be the means of destruction. The jagged edge flashes silver against the blue sky, soon it will turn red. The blade drops, slices, the boy squirms, cries out, coughs and bleeds to death all over his father's hunched, weeping body. At least in my mind's eye. On the page there's good news – thank God for good news –it's a test, it's the millionaire question – the *Mastermind* final – God doesn't want a dead sacrifice, he wants a living one. It's the same old Catch, the one between 21 and 23. The greatest act of freewill is to choose to give it up. Ask not what your planet can do for you but what you can do for your planet. Another Father did that later, and another Son took the fall. Another boy lay down on the slab and let the knife fall. Stepped in front of the president and took the bullet. Pushed me out of the way of the speeding train and left his own blood on the tracks.

The planet's never been the same since.

So Isaac is spared, marries wily Rebekah and they have the twins.

Jacob and Esau.

My brother is an hairy man, but I am a smooth man.

So says the old sketch. But that's only the start of it. Sibling rivalry rears its ugly head again. These biblical brats sure paved the way for today's renegades. James Dean had nothing on dear Jake. Swindling his brother's inheritance was only the start of it. Egged on by sharp-as-nails Rebekah, he cons his old man and leaves home with vengeance snapping at his heels. This rebel has a cause and he can run. Like the wind. Jacob knows how to duck and dive, how to wheel and deal. Taking up with his uncle Laban soon proves an astute move. He learns quickly, fathoms how to prosper. But uncle Laban is his mother's brother, he certainly has the devious streak. Oh, it's all there in Genesis 29. Maybe Jake got it from his mother's side, or maybe from his father Isaac, or maybe ancient Abraham. All of them were no strangers to spinning a yarn. Survival was paramount, and if the wife could be a useful tool . . .

Talking of wives, Jake soon fell in love, I mean really fell in love, not just because it was a useful device. He tripped headlong for Rachel. Beautiful, sexy, intelligent Rachel. And when Laban offered to pay Jake, this grasping man could think of only one thing. Miss Right, please. Sure, just work seven years for me. Seven years! Grief, two weeks seems forever these days. Seven years of nodding, winking and nudge nudging. But he holds on and keeps his suit pressed. Then the whammy – Jake should have seen it coming, shouldn't have fallen for it, after all, this is Laban, your mother's brother, your own uncle. Trickery's his middle name. Too late.

'Do you take this woman to be your lawful wedded wife?'

'Sure, after all she's the girl of my dreams.'

'Well, not quite, she has got great eyes, but . . .'

Jacob snatches away the veil. Surprise! It's not Rachel. He's married Leah.

Lucky you can have more than one wife.

Unlucky that you're dealing with your Uncle Laban.

Seven more years hard labour. Another sister, another wedding.

'Do you take this woman?'

'What do you think? I've only been waiting a decade and a half . . .'

By the time Jacob plucks up enough courage to head for home, he's got more sheep than New Zealand and almost as many wives as Henry VIII. Twelve kids in tow too.

'Are we nearly there yet, dad?'

You can hear it now.

'Yes son, we're nearly there, which is unfortunate, cos your old man's in no hurry. Your Uncle Esau is likely to garrotte him on sight. Let's break for camp for just one more night. I'd like to enjoy the use of my legs a little longer.'

So they break for camp for one last night of freedom. And in true father Abraham fashion, Jacob decides to put the women in the firing line. And then he gets the shock of his life.

He's just dozing off, just got his head settled nicely on the pillow, just watching the orange sunset glow dying gracefully beyond the horizon, listening to the buzz of flies and the rhythmic sawing of the crickets, when . . . there's the sudden sound of a twig breaking. And hours later, another crack rings out – this time it's not a twig breaking but a hip. Oh dear, it's his.

It's 2.34 a.m. I've finished my tea and started on a half-empty tube of Pringles. The new day is a long way away but I'm limping already. I've limped for a long time. Is that a blessing? Or a curse?

Everybody limps, surely. One way or another. Damaged hips, hearts, lives, spirits. Can that ever be a blessing? Better not start on that road too far, it sounds too much like sadism to picture divine hands cracking ribs so they can then be of support to a broken body. This is a tough one.

So, Jacob meets his Maker and finds himself wrestling with a Stranger. He was on such poor terms with God that when they met it took him all night to realise he was in the presence of Greatness. But he got there in the end and when he finally met his brother, he was a wreck. And his brother dug deep and forgave him. His twelve sons, by four different mothers, grow up to be a raggle-taggle bunch, as good at infighting as they are at raising sheep. And along comes our kid. Joseph. Smart, good-looking, cocky, naive Joseph. Airhead and regular dreamer. Dad's favourite and spoilt brat. The sun shines out of his . . . well actually it doesn't, it bows down and worships him. In your dreams, mate.

Sometimes the Bible seems full of privileged people. I mean, Jacob comes back from exile with more meat than McDonalds. Admittedly he earned it all, but wealth was in the blood, great granddaddy Abe had oceans of opulence. Sure he was an old-age traveller but he didn't travel light. He came with baggage. I realise, as I fill my mouth with too many Pringles, that I've often thought of these stories as being about poor struggling waifs – the inhabitants of English soapland. Maybe I need to change continents. Think *West Wing* rather than *Coronation Street*. *Friends* rather than *Fools and Horses*.

The thought of all that meat puts me in mind of the leftover bacon sitting in Joel's fridge. A bacon sarnie wouldn't go amiss right now, the Pringles are nearly all gone. Easy enough to throw a few rashers in a pan. Oh, and there are one or two eggs left too, and some sausages and mushrooms. I discover it's not too long a walk from a bacon butty to a full fry-up. I shut the door, rev the stove and set to work. Jacob swapped his birthright for a mess of pottage – was that the 2000 BC equivalent of a full monty? I gaze on the sight and wonder. Succulent rosy tomatoes, glossy mushrooms oozing juice and flavour, a couple of dazzling white sunshiney eggs, sizzling brown-shouldered sausages, all topped off with a couple of slices of golden brown fried bread. Heaven. And it may well send me there.

Jacob finished his days in Egypt, though he was buried back in Canaan. Along the way he experienced famine, family breakdown and the loss of his favourite son. His life was chequered but he made it in the end. The cheat, the grabber, the wheeler dealer who did his unlevel best to manipulate God. In the end he lost the fight but won the prize. A quick gander at Hebrews 11 tells the startling tale. This loser became a hero up there with the rest of them – and his greatest act of faith, the one he went down in history for, was to believe that his wayward, misfit sons would somehow spawn the people of God. Which they did in spite of being losers and criminals. Maybe that's why Jesus had such a soft spot for lowlife.

I finish my fry-up, leave the kitchen looking like the Somme and limp back up to bed. I think it's time I went home.

23. Don't Leave Me This Way

Luke 24:50–51; Acts 1:6–12

They walk up the mountain in relative silence. Thomas chunters on about this and that but he's always full of hot air, that's his problem, he just says it out, brain lacking the ability to get in the right gear and all that. Sadly he doesn't have a mute button.

There's a strange atmosphere, their heads are thick with mixed messages. It's been a bizarre time, forty days of elation and mystery and madness.

Why are they doing this now? Why is there such a heavy mood lurking; wisps of doubt and confusion snaking between them? Maybe Jesus is going to meet Moses and Elijah again? Maybe he's taking them all along this time. Thomas'll be pleased, he was well miffed at missing out last time. He's missed out a lot on the miraculous, has old Thomas, always in the wrong place at the wrong time. Maybe this'll be a good one after all, a bright sunshiny day, maybe they're all going up there to meet their Maker. They'll never come down again. Rumours and news stories will be all that's left of them. *Twelve men lost on tragic mountain trip. No sign of the bodies. Anyone with information please come forward.*

They're at the top. Jesus stops, turns and studies them.

'This is it,' he says, and he sounds as if it's difficult to say it.

'This is what?' asks Peter. 'Are you gonna do it now? Kick out the Romans and restore Israel – true government and rough justice and all that? Is that what this is about?'

Jesus and John both shake their heads.

'No, Peter, this is not what it's about.'

'How does he know? How does John know?'

'Because we talked. We've talked a lot. I'd have talked to you but you rarely listen. This is the end, Peter, well the end of the beginning. There's plenty more to come . . .'

Then, in mid-sentence he just breaks off, just like that and walks round, bear-hugging them one by one. Halfway round the circle he breaks down and Thaddeus and Andrew have to support him for a while. The confusion increases. You can cut it with a knife. Then he picks himself up and moves on, more bear-hugs and muttered goodbyes.

Peter's the last.

'Don't go. Don't do this.'

Peter's fighting to keep himself under control. Suddenly it's all hit him, he knows what is happening and he doesn't like it one bit.

Jesus looks at him, his eyes wet and his face strained. He forces a smile.

'We've been through a lot, Peter,' he says. 'Would you have left those nets if you'd have known?'

Peter can't reply. He nods, then shakes his head, then nods, then just shrugs.

'Don't go,' he says again but his voice is barely a whisper.

'I have to.'

Tears slip down Peter's face and he fists them away quickly. Jesus is crying now too. This is the worst moment of Peter's life.

'What'll happen to us? We can't do this without you. Look at us, we're useless.'

Peter's staring at the ground, fighting back the terrible volcano that's building inside his chest. He must stay strong, he won't look an idiot.

Jesus places a hand on the back of Peter's head and lifts his face.

'Remember what I said,' he whispers, 'you're not useless. I meant what I said that day I spotted you fishing. You can do this.'

Jesus wipes his face on the back of his hand and sniffs loudly. He composes himself.

'Look after these guys. Keep them strong, keep them focused, share some of that rock that's in there.'

He punches Peter's chest and they both smile.

'But we don't know what to do. You've always been the leader.'

Jesus shakes his head.

'Not any more – it's over to you now, mate. You use that talent – you've been desperate to take control anyway. This is your moment. And you'll know what to do, because soon my strength, my energy and my direction will come back to you. It'll be right here pumping through your thick skull. And then believe me, there'll be no stopping you.'

Peter shakes his head, he doesn't believe it. He just wants this appalling experience to end.

Jesus turns and walks a few feet away. Peter risks a glance around, he's not the only grown man crying up there right now. And Thomas is angry too.

'Things were just getting better,' he blurts out, spit spattering his chin as he jabs out the words.

Jesus nods.

'Thomas – you have no idea how much better it will be when I'm gone.'

'That's ridiculous.'

Jesus laughs. 'Of course it is. But my Father's chosen the ridiculous to overthrow the reasonable.'

He blows out his cheeks and points down the hill.

'Get back to the city and wait. My Father is going to send you everything you need, then you'll be off all over the place. But don't rush it, wait for my Father.'

'Yea but . . .'

Peter can't finish. His mouth just sits open, sagging like a broken hinge. Everyone's staring upwards into the sun now. They're still staring five minutes later.

'Did you see what I . . .'

'Yea.'

'Wow!'

One of them laughs. Peter stares at him, then another joins in. Suddenly they're all laughing. They shouldn't be, they don't know why, but they're pointing at the sky and falling about.

'What are you doing?'

They look at the strangers. Two men from the city.

'You wouldn't believe us if we told you.'

'Yes we would – but you heard him. What are you doing here? Standing around gawping into the sky? Get back to the city and wait. He won't be back for a while yet. Go on!'

This day has been weird and this is the strangest occurrence of all, but they saunter down the hill anyway, pushing and shoving each other, still laughing, still bantering, still confused.

Leaving Joel's is always tough but this time is harder than ever. I pack up in sombre fashion – there's not a huge amount to pack anyway but I make the most of it. I find Joel downstairs tapping away on his Apple Mac. We neither of us want to say goodbye but I know he's keen for me to get back to some kind of reconciliatory reunion with my wife. We're not sure whether or not to hug so we hang about by the back door, kicking at the concrete and doing our best to make small talk, something neither of us is good at.

Eventually there's no other reason not to say goodbye so we pat each other's shoulders, shake each other's hands and give each other a mutant kind of hug. The kind of hug that's more like holding a bag of cement to your chest while carting it from one space to another. I finally get in the car and I'm off, down that sweeping gravel drive, leaving my best friend and that awesome house for another year. It's bound to be 365 days before I set eyes on them both again. At least.

As ever the first part of my journey is rife with memories, not just from the past three days, but the last thirty years. Then the management light comes on and suddenly I'm plunged into chaos. I have no idea it actually is the management light until I pull into a lay-by and look it up, but it is and I'm in trouble.

It's only a tiny light but it's blazing a dangerous red – glaring at me from its vantage point right there on the dashboard. What can this mean? Do I have another five hundred miles in the engine or five hundred yards? Dare I risk going on or should I go back? If Marco Polo had been put off by a little red light, he'd never have made China, Drake wouldn't have scuppered the Armada, Scott wouldn't have trudged to the South Pole and Cook wouldn't have enjoyed Hawaii. Actually Cook didn't enjoy Hawaii and might well have welcomed a management light to stop him ever setting foot on those shores. But that's another story. You know what I'm saying. Where's my spirit of adventure? Where's the soul of Ernie Shackleton? Surely I can put up with a little red light for a few miles. Am I a wimp or a warrior?

A big strong boy or a big girl's blouse? I fish out the phone and call the RAC. Oh, it's the big blouse then.

'Sixty minutes? What d'you mean sixty minutes? It's practically the crack of dawn. Everyone's still in the land of nod. How can there be a backlog already?'

Well there is. So I get out of my car, case the joint and spot just the thing that warms a lonely traveller's heart. And amazingly, at 10.30 in the morning in the middle of nowhere, it's open.

A local village pub.

24. Free Food and Gas Bills

2 Corinthians 3:1–3

Paul snaps his fingers and grasps for the right words. He's concerned that he's bragging again, in his zest for the faith he often branches off into realms of self-adulation. But it's never meant to sound that way. It really isn't. He just goes off on one sometimes.

What can he use to bring them back to what he means? The prophets were so good at this, David too. Stories, analogies, shocking imagery and stunning visions. Right now he'd kill for a valley of dry bones or a boat full of animals under a sky full of rainbow. All he has is the scratch, scratch, scratching of his scribe's pen. The irritating scraping as the poor old man attempts to keep up with the prophet's ramblings. Wait a minute. Pens. Pens and letters, that might work. Paul snaps his fingers and hurries over and grabs the scribe's shoulder.

'Try this,' he says, and his dictation takes on a new urgency.

'Are we beginning again to tell you how good we are? Because we don't mean to do that. Some people need to bring letters of recommendation with them or ask you to write letters of recommendation for them. But you are my letter. It's you I'm praising up here. The only letter of recommendation we need is you yourselves! People look at you and they're amazed at what they see. You're different, you're changing, you're more honest, there's hope in your eyes. You struggle, yes, you're not always peaceful, but you're moving somewhere now. Your lives are like a letter written in our hearts, your day-to-day living tells the story, proclaims the faith. The message is writ large in you much more powerfully than in a million sermons. And it's easy for everyone to read, you don't have to be literate or educated; it's as clear as day. My letters are often as clear as mud – but your lives shout the story. Clearly, you are a letter from Christ prepared by us. It is not written down with pen and ink, but with the Spirit of the living God. It is carved not on stone, but inscribed on human hearts.'

Paul scratches his head and looks at his old friend.

'What do you think?' he asks.

The old man shrugs. 'I don't know,' he says, 'I only got as far as the second sentence, you went too fast.'

The Hangman's Hood is empty apart from three locals and a dog. They all turn and stare at me as I shuffle sheepishly in. It's one of those 'What you doing here?' kind of looks that English pubs excel in.

Quiz night in here probably leads off with – *Question 1: What you looking at? Question 2: I said – what you looking at?*

I force a weak grin, to which the dog growls and the people don't smile. Thankfully the landlady is brighter and cheerier than the rest and comes out right on cue to pour me a pint and tell me that her name's Judy. We chat for a bit about my Ford Money-pit and how bad the weather's been – even though it's been remarkably good, then I take my pint and sidle over to a blood-red vinyl-covered armchair beside a freshly made fire just beginning to blaze in the huge slate-trimmed hearth. The walls nearby are lined with fat oak shelves groaning under the weight of hundreds and hundreds of leather-bound books. I catch sight of *Treasure Island*, *Peter Pan* and *Alice in Wonderland*, plus every Enid Blyton title in the known universe. No sign of the good book but it's okay, I smuggled in my own. So I pull out the volume that certainly isn't for kids. Noah's ark, Daniel's lions, David's giant? Kids' stories? You're kidding me, right?

I take a swig of Guinness, fish out my black book and relax. A good mate of mine reckons quaffing Guinness is like supping solid concrete. He may be right, especially this early in the day. The same good mate also reckons we're the best bit of multimedia God has. Nothing beats your face, your ears, your eyes, your hands and feet, your ear lobe, small intestine or double chin, he says, when it comes to communicating God. We are the most effective page in God's worldwide web. For good or ill, we can demonstrate many things powerfully, and people recall masses more of what we do than what we say. Words pass, sermons fade, conversations wither and die but these three remain – faces, hands and limbs – and the greatest of these . . . is yours.

Another local comes in and the whole place lights up; it's as if Santa Claus has come to town. He's short, plump and sports a leather biker's jacket. Much laughing and swearing heralds his arrival. This is at around 11.00, and the dour locals suddenly morph into the Waltons. They look younger, brighter and even the dog smiles. I find it difficult to tear my eyes away from the spectacle, I'm not sure I've ever witnessed such a reaction to one man before. He looks for all the world like the local equivalent of Harry Secombe and I expect him to break into *The Ying Tong Song* at any moment. He orders a pint of real ale, slaps a few backs and points towards the gents. Everyone laughs and the place rocks with hilarity as laughing boy heads for the loo.

As he passes me on his merry way a stylophone rendition of the Indiana Jones theme rings out and I realise it's his mobile. He chortles, nods at me and pulls it from his jacket, and that's when I catch sight of the dog collar round his neck. Not a Scooby Doo kind of dog collar – a Father Ted/Ian Paisley kind of dog collar (you choose the denomination of preference). Either way it turns out Santa Claus is the vicar.

'He's a sweet fella,' Judy says to me as she comes over to hurl another cumbersome log on the fire.

'He's the vicar?'

'Oh yea, but don't let that put you off – he's not very religious really. I mean he does services and all, but not many go, that's why he comes down here. He's often out the back playing dominoes with the grandads or having his ear bent by one of the farmer's lads. He's dunking my granddaughter next week so a lot of us'll go along to that.'

'Dunking?'

'Christening. Bit of a posh do so we'll make an effort and lots of the village will be there. He's picked a few favourite hymns – *Plough the fields and scatter, All things bright and beautiful, Nearer my God to thee*, that sort of thing. He'll do a lovely job. He's great with kids and oldies. Then we've got a bit of a do back here afterwards. Next Thursday it is, pop in if you're around. What's that you're reading? One of ours is it?'

She nods towards the jammed shelves.

'No, it's . . .'

Crunch time. Do I admit it?

'Oh sorry – gotta go, his highness is back and I need to top up his ale.'

The local hero passes me on the way back from the gents and nods at me. He jabs a portly finger at the book.

'Try Leviticus – it's riveting,' he says and everyone at the bar laughs.

For a while I wonder if I'm really awake. It just seems like I'm in a sitcom. Jolly, ale-swigging, leather-clad, domino-playing, Indiana Jones-loving clergymen really do exist. At least in this village.

Do the locals know more about Jesus because of him? Who can say? They probably have more idea of how Jesus might behave in a modern pub. Clearly he's no bad ad for the faith. Definitely a great living letter – he's a sort of *Congratulations you've won free food for the rest of your born days* kind of letter – I think I'm more of a *Bad news your gas bill's just gone up by 400%* kind of letter.

I turn back to my little black book and stare at one of Paul's many extremely long communications. Was Paul the life and soul of the party? I doubt it. People were probably removing him from their party lists as fast as they were receiving his fifteen-page letters (double-sided). I guess if they'd had email he'd have been sending them round as e-pistles. But Jesus was a party animal. He was always getting into trouble for being way too frivolous, and whichever way you cut it, making a tanker full of wine at *that* wedding was always gonna result in a lot of headaches the next morning. I wonder if he'd have been accused of giving the people what they wanted? Pandering to their needs? Playing the popularity card? No doubt the Pharisees thought so.

But not on the day after he fed twenty thousand people. He often fell out with the Pharisees but on this occasion he fell out with everybody. This was the day after the big miracle, the day revival should have broken out, the day the seafood sandwich circus came to town. Goodness knows how many pitched up that next morning, cos no doubt they all went home and bragged to their friends and family about how amazing this Jesus is and how they should have been there. So thousands upon thousands of fish-hungry punters must have showed up with their little jugs of hollandaise sauce. And did he have a shock for them.

'Do it again, Jesus!'

'Do the magic bread thing!'

'Conjure the cod!'

'Show me the mornay!'

But Jesus wouldn't. He'd refused in the wilderness and he refused now.

'Oh, go on, I've brought all me mates. I'll look a right idiot if you don't do it. They don't believe me – prove it to them. Go on, do the bread trick.'

And in an effort to bring some semblance of sanity, Jesus points them all to Moses – and the kind of bread that can feed the soul.

'Yea, we like Moses!' they say. 'He did the magic bread thing too. Do the magic bread thing, Jesus! Go on. I've brought me granny.'

All the people can think of is their stomachs – they can't get a grip on their souls.

'The truth is,' Jesus says, 'you didn't see the sign – you only saw the miracle. You didn't see the sign of twenty thousand people all sitting down together breaking bread and sharing food. Prostitutes, priests, men, women, poor and rich, old and young, leaders and fol-lowers, all sitting and eating together. A sign of the king-dom, a sign of the future day when that will be the norm. You couldn't see it and you still refuse to, so I won't make any more bread. Make it yourselves. You can cook. I'm not a divine baker. Go home and make your own, and when you're ready, come back and we'll discuss bread that doesn't rot, food that doesn't go mouldy. Open your eyes – open your eyes! Look for the signs of the kingdom!'

And twenty thousand people wandered off with their stomachs rumbling and their friends muttering about how it didn't really happen. People probably just shared their packed lunches.

So what about Reverend Jolly here in the Hangman's Hood – is he just giving folks what they want, is he playing the popular card, or is he being a great bit of multimedia? Sooner or later the hard questions always come up, push always comes to shove – maybe he's just happy to wait for later rather than sooner.

I realise my hour's up and I stand up to get back to the car.

Judy watches me pick up my little battered book and slip it into my back pocket.

She winks at me as I place my empty pint on the bar.

'I thought it was the Bible,' she says, 'you just know, don't you. Bibles have that look about them. You can always tell.'

'Ever read it?' I ask.

She shakes her head. 'Well, I did, when I was little, at Sunday school you know. I always loved that one about the lost coin. That woman searching high and low and then throwing a party when she found it.' She laughs. 'Probably the sort of thing I'd do. Find a penny and spend a pound.'

I nod and laugh with her, then she winks again and I leave the Hangman's Hood as sheepishly as I came in.

25. Dawn of the Dead

John 20:1–18

The ground shudders a little. Then it rattles again and a few trees buckle and topple over. All goes quiet before the final sudden explosion and rocks crack and tumble. And one rock in particular, a huge fat stone that's supposed to keep the dead from the living. While it's still dark, this single stone twitches, fractures and rolls away from the cave it's intended to be covering.

A man steps into the grey shadowy doorway, stretching and gasping for breath. He sighs and yawns and then laughs. The dawn begins to break and faint rays of orange sun highlight the holes in his hands, the glow shows through the gaps in his flesh, lighting up spots on the wall of the cave behind him. He wipes deathly sleep from his eyes so that he can see straight. The world has never looked so good to him. Everything's changed now. If only Adam could see this new day, all that regret in his heart would be swept away. Still, it may be too late for Adam but it's perfect for the rest of his family.

There's the sound of a footfall in the garden. Jesus stops, listens, then nips into the bushes. He must pick his moment carefully, he doesn't want to shock her, but the potential for laughter is too good to miss. He waits, hardly containing himself, the Son of God hiding in the bushes. It's a moment of redemption for Adam and Eve.

Mary goes in, screams and comes out sobbing: she's angry and broken and confused. He tiptoes close to her. She hears him, starts and swings round.

Oh! She thinks he's the gardener. He so wanted to make her jump. Jump and leap and fall about laughing, but he quickly realises she's too fragile for that. So he says the one thing that will reassure her. He says her name. Her eyes split wide like halved grapefruits. He judges it perfectly.

'Teacher? Is it . . . Is it?'

She stares, shock etched across her face.

He waits, smiles, nods and she hurls herself at him. The fun will have to wait, this is a moment for reunion and reassurance. Soon he'll be cropping up all over the place, stepping through walls and appearing on beaches. But for now he needs to be gentle. Resurrection is an awesome thing – it needs to be handled carefully.

The RAC man is courteous and quiet and looks more like an extra from *The Office*. He studies my engine as if it's a sheet of accountancy figures. He shows no emotion and won't let me in on the secret of what's wrong with The Management.

'Reminds me of Hale and Pace,' I joke pointing at the exposed engine. 'You know, *The Management*, Ron and Ron, remember?'

He doesn't. He's a decade too young.

'I need to reset it,' he says.

'Reset what?'

'The management.'

'And will that fix it?'

'No, it'll reset it so the light goes off.'

'And what does that mean?'

'It means the light won't be on when you drive.'

Rrrrrrrright.

I leave him to it and wander into a nearby church-yard. Apart from the whitewashed Hangman's Hood, this eleventh-century church is the only building for miles around. I know it's so old because it's inscribed across the twenty-first-century Day-Glo noticeboard. A crowd of crickets fiddle away in the background: they must really like this mid-morning weather, their back legs are rasping so fast I'm surprised they don't spontaneously combust. The churchyard is littered with an untidy jigsaw of tombstones. Granite crosses, squares and arches compete for attention in this nettle-infested corner of England. There's something comforting about the overgrown character of the place. I can kid myself that life's not really changing at such a breakneck pace after all.

I once did one of those personality tests to find out who I am – Mires Boggs I think it was called – I came out as an introvert which is why I'd rather wander round graveyards with dead people than stand around chin-wagging with live ones. You answer a million questions and they sum you up in four words. If I remember correctly I'm a sagittarian, introverted, cockeyed, know-it-all. S. I. C. K. for short.

Something like that anyway. It didn't really change my life but it explained why I always find myself in the kitchen at parties.

I wander from one tombstone to the next and I'm gob-smacked by the level of affection in this place. If you want to know what love is, have elevenses in a cemetery.

We will always miss you.
You were everything to me.
They are together forever.
Reunited at last.
She was a perfect mother and a loving wife.
We love you dad.

I hope and long for the day when we shall meet again.

The epitaphs go on and on and on. And okay it maybe glassy-eyed coffin-love, but it still speaks volumes. The dead cry out from this hallowed ground and if I have any sense I'll sit up and take notice. Is it just after-the-fact affection? We love to praise our politicians once they're no longer in power. Saints only become immortal when they've ceased being mortal. The majority of heroes are dead ones. But there's definitely something powerful about this place. We miss people when they're gone. We appreciate them when we can't tell them that we do. It brings out the gratitude in us. It's hard to say thank you face to face – so we do it with a chisel and a hammer. These people were loved, for better or worse. And many of the messages are from wives to husbands and husbands to wives. Or children to parents and, in the worst-case scenarios, parents to children.

I find myself thinking about the one tombstone you won't find here. The Man they buried who wrecked his own funeral. Just as they're proofreading the obituary, Jesus comes back and demands a rewrite. Bang! That's how to make people jump. Wait till they're creeping through a dark cemetery at dawn, then leap out and tap them on the shoulder.

I met a guy recently who reckoned Easter Sunday must have been the most disappointing day of Jesus' life. Where was everybody? He'd told them he was coming back. Where were they all? Where were the streamers and the champagne bottles? The place was deserted. Just a couple of angels and two sleeping soldiers.

When he died there was a lot of razzmatazz. Graves opened up, bodies clawed their way out of the earth and countless recomposing figures were seen knocking on their relatives' doors.

'Who's there? Uncle Blastus? But you've been dead ten years. Is it you making that dreadful smell?'

I find myself standing in front of a large granite cross mounted magnificently on a raised white grave. Well-kept fresh flowers litter the clean stone and a dozen names decorate the collective resting place, all sharing the same surname. I read the caption out loud and instantly feel foolish for doing so.

> For the Lord himself will come down from heaven with a commanding shout, with the call of the archangel, and with the trumpet call of God. First, all the Christians who have died will rise from their graves.

I look around to check that no one has heard my outburst, but I'm alone here apart, of course, from a thousand departed souls and a hundred happy crickets. If I recall correctly, this passage is preceded and followed by the news that all those who have died and gone to heaven will return with Jesus and everyone still alive will rise up to meet him. So what with graves opening, dead people returning and live ones flying up, it'll need the best air traffic controllers heaven can afford to avoid a massive pile-up in the stratosphere. Still, by then no-one will be able to die or get injured, so it should be all right. Just a lot of harmless mid-air collisions. From space it could look like the pinball game to end all pinball games. I sometimes wonder if turbulence aboard your average flight is the result of cannon-balling a few guardian angels out on their tour of duty; either that or it's down to bored pilots – 'Let's spice this flight up a bit, waggle your controls for a few minutes and we'll tell 'em it's a bit of bad weather.'

It's weird, though, isn't it? The thought of all those tombs cracking open – like the night of the living dead all over the planet.

Right beside this grave of graves there's another plot, unkempt, colourless and alone. But I suddenly realise I'm staring at a name I know very well. Mr Andrew Teak. I'll never forget that name. The man who inspired me and believed in me in my early days at school. No one forgets a good teacher: well, I'll certainly never forget him. I check the dates and realise he was only 59 when he died. Could it really be him? The age would fit and I do recall him moving away from our village. I'm suddenly sorry that I can never go back and visit him and tell him what I'm doing now. This man invested in me, he trusted me, gave me undeserved responsibility, listened to me and lent me the first book I loved. I guess I'll never forget this moment. Mr Teak shouldn't be dead, he should be alive and still inspiring other people. Teachers are another breed, aren't they? They're large people who inhabit another world. They're superhuman. They tower above you and know everything you need to know. They appear on Monday and disappear on Friday. They don't die and end up in a little grave in a little village.

When Jesus rose it was a relatively quiet, subtle affair. Apart from the planet-shattering earthquake, of course. I have watched countless films about Jesus and every one of them is rubbish when it comes to the resurrection. Apparently when Jesus comes back from the dead, he looks very serious and he walks in slow motion. Oh really? So what's all that stuff about walking through walls and surprising people on a regular basis? I think the word mischievous comes to mind, don't you? Why do we confuse holiness with seriousness? Why do we think that a risen Jesus couldn't crack jokes, surprise people on a regular basis and bring an awful lot of laughter? Death's over, for goodness sake. That's gotta be good cause for a belly laugh. It doesn't get any better than this – it's the ultimate feel-good ending.

26. Sidewhacked

Luke 2:21–35

The little couple shuffle into the Temple. They look so, so small next to the colossal stonework, beneath the massive arches. Joseph's trying to bluster his way and look more confident than he feels, but it's all front.

He's not been the same since that angel splashed him round the face and brought him up short with the truth about his only Son. Since then, he's felt permanently wrong-footed, every rug has been jerked from under him. All that talk of angelic choirs and highly favoured women, it just bewilders him. Shepherds appearing bright-eyed and breathless, spewing stories of goodwill and peace on earth. It was hardly peaceful that night. It was all blood and screams, and wondering if his wife was gonna live. He's a working man, a practical blue-collar guy. A bloke who loves wood and stone: what on earth is he to do with all this ethereal messianic baby stuff? He slips a cautious arm around Mary. She seems to grow in confidence with each passing day, especially now that she's regaining her strength after the difficult birth. She gets bigger and he gets smaller. All the light is on her. Shepherds, visitors, family – she gets all the attention, he may as well not exist. They say the father's day is nine months before the mother's day – but even that's not true in this case. Having your first baby is always a shock to the system, his old man told him that, but this one's really sidewhacked him.

Then the old man steps out of the shadows and something starts to change. He's wrinkled and hunched and one of his eyes is dodgy. His hands shake and his voice sounds like a frog with laryngitis.

'May I?' he asks, gesturing towards the child.

From behind him there's an even older person, a tiny bird-like woman, with twinkling eyes and deep lines in her brow. Between them they smuggle the baby from Mary's arms. Mary shrinks a little as she loses her child, as if her new-found strength is in direct correlation with her new-born Son, but the ancient couple are hardly likely to make off with the bundle. They'd pass out before they broke a sweat.

The old man's appearance is deceptive though. His body may be broken from years of spine-crunching work but his spirit is as straight as a Roman spear, and twice as sharp. He may not smell too good, he may slur his words from time to time, he may be invisible to most people but this guy won't need angels or stars to inform him about this significant birth. He'll show more faith than any younger man. He's been impatient for this moment, ranted at the skies about it, grumbled at passers-by. How long, how long? When? When ? When?

And people have written him off as mad. But today he's more sane than anyone else on the planet. Anyone except his old friend Anna. They'll both be long dead before this child is out of first-century nappies, but they've plotted for this day for too long, psyched themselves up for this moment. They won't let it pass unannounced. Something inside him explodes when he sees those tiny fingers and feels those mini feet beating against his chest.

'This screaming child,' he rasps, 'this screaming child will one day cry out and silence all the other voices.

Many people will rise and fall because of him. And you, Mary, you will feel the sharp end of a sword digging deep into your soul, cutting right through to your heart. It won't be easy nurturing a boy who's come to nurture you. This boy will clear away all the rubbish that's talked about God, and distil the truth into one single moment. Secrets and lies will be unearthed in his presence. You two are blessed – but I don't envy you. Especially not at my age, I'm way past the years of broken nights and crack-of-dawn mornings.'

Later, while Mary and Anna compare notes, Joe takes Simeon to one side and confides in him. There's something about this wheezy old man that smacks of integrity. He's not threatening, he's not cocky, he's not pretending – what you see is what you get. Joe doesn't know him from Adam but that makes it all the easier. He'll probably never see him again, so right now he's the perfect friend. He'd never admit it to the Nazareth guild of carpenters but Joe's scared; this baby's got him on the back foot, and with this guy he's not afraid to show it. The old man listens, nods, grunts and tugs at the rough snags of white beard on his chin. And in the end, when Joe's finished frothing, the old man smiles, pats him on the back, and in his rasping slurred voice says, 'You'll be all right son, you'll be all right.'

And though there's nothing spectacular about the advice, somehow Joe knows that it's true.

The car is fixed and ready to go. I thank the RAC guy, the *Office* extra, and he looks a little embarrassed at my profuse gratitude. I wouldn't normally be so enthusiastic towards a stranger but I'm inspired by my moments in the graveyard. For a few short minutes I don't care what anyone thinks of me. Life is short, too short to be inhibited about the good things. He may think I'm mad but I don't care. Tomorrow I'll care, but not today.

He gets in his car and I get in my car and we both pull away.

Life is sweet for a while, the dead have restored my faith in life. Then the management light comes on again. Oh great. Should I bother? Should I care? I wrestle with myself for a while about it, then give up. If the car blows up, it blows up. I pull over and call my wife. I talk to her about the last two days, she tells me about the kids, I admit it's been good, she does the same. The kids have had fun with their cousins. That's a relief. We hang up while the going's good. I flip to the beginning of Luke, I'm looking for something to match the sudden hope I feel coursing through my veins. Make the most of it before it seeps out again. I happen upon the strange bit of Christmas. The old guy who somehow spots Jesus without the aid of stars or angels or dreams. There's something quirky yet utterly feelgood about this story. He's so happy about his dreams coming true that he's prepared to die now. He's not morbid, he's not suicidal, he's just satisfied. Things have turned out well and nothing can get better than this. Who's more satisfied – the man with seven million dollars or the man with seven kids? Quite clearly the man with seven kids – cos he doesn't want any more. That was Simeon that day. There was nothing more for him in life. He'd seen it all now.

This is an astonishing moment – the greatest act of faith in the Christmas story. Angels from the realms of glory and stars of wonder stars of light may have gone down in history and make for some raucous back-row singing, but I figure it's not those bright lights that we need today. It's the spirit of Simeon. An old man sees two people and a baby in the cold light of day and he believes. He hears a whisper in his soul and he hangs on to it. This is the Christmas baby, small, insignificant, born on the night when plenty of other children broke into this world, nothing about him to make him stand out or draw us to him. The boy who will lead us from darkness to light.

Last Christmas I saw two versions of this timeless tale. One featured Bugs Bunny, runny noses and my four-year-old. The other had a cast of thousands, real camels and the girl from *Whale Rider*. Both were funny and moving and took a lot of work. It made me wonder which Nativity was more trouble – the first one or those we've been staging ever since. Sadly, my wife and I were the only ones watching the one with the real camels. Was that something to do with a misconception about the Immaculate Conception? The night we saw Bond the cinema was jam-packed. James or Jesus? Seems most people choose James. Why? Both are heroes. Both do incredible things.

Did Joe take heart from meeting this old guy? Were his fears about the future allayed? Soon he'd be boarding a camel himself and tearing off into the Egyptian night. My guess is those two old folks who shuffled over in the Temple provided as much if not more assurance than all the shepherds in the Promised Land. They weren't there for the glory of it – they were there because this thing was real. It meant something and they didn't need Christmas lights and angelic carol singers to bolster their excitement. They saw a tiny scrap of heaven and they believed. Happy are those who follow in their footsteps.

27. The Hitcher

Loosely based on Luke 22:39–46; Matthew 27:38–50

One dark night, just around Easter time, the forces of darkness gathered on earth to do battle for the life of a human soul.

Dark, brooding shadows hung in the air, like thick, black storm clouds. Demons clad as armed soldiers, fallen angels in priests' robes; all of them devils in disguise.

Swords flashed in the moonlight, torches raged with a fearsome blaze against the black cavern of night, and an all-consuming fire shone in the eyes of those plotting nothing but downfall.

And beyond, in the starry distance, the clear eyes of God watched and waited. The bared, blackened teeth of the enemy, the poisoned gums drawn back, the spitting, incessant rain of curses and the whispered threats; he saw and heard them all.

And finally, eventually, God spoke.

'Enough,' he said, 'enough. No longer will we tolerate the forces of madness, no longer will I allow the twin spirits of chaos and anarchy to stalk the streets of my people.'

And so, at the critical moment, just as dark spirits raised withered hands to tear the life from another helpless human soul . . . at that moment God intervened.

There was no mighty battle, no bloody crushing, no days of swordplay and archery. God lowered his hand and in one single moment swept the fearsome foe aside. Off and into the abyss. For good.

Every last one of the seeking spirits and dark devils dispensed with, cast aside, no more to be suffered and tolerated.

And a single man stood alive and well on planet earth.

A single man stood safe and secure in the shadow of an unmarked cross.

The watching people, the millions who gathered to view the spectacle, cheered and clapped and whistled. At last God had proved his point.

At last the waiting was over.

At last he was real.

The young man shook his head and quietly walked away from the jubilant crowd, taking one last glance at the silent, redundant cross.

He had been rescued by a visible, mighty God.

But a billion others had not; humanity was still forever lost.

I'm back on the road and I drive for an hour. At some point I veer off the road and grab a healthy portable lunch: a cheese and onion pasty and four packs of jaffa cakes. And I'm off again. Then I start passing the hitch-hikers and I get the guilty feeling. Here I am with an empty vehicle, corroding my way through another bit of the ozone and the least I could do is share the experience with someone else. I glance at the empty seats. I came away with very little so I could travel light, yet the car's full, there's stuff everywhere. CD cases, Yorkie wrappers, jumpers, bags, empty jaffa cake boxes, maps, pasty crumbs and three old rotting apple cores that came to light when we removed the children's car seats three days ago. I meant to clean them up immediately but they're still here, fur and all, sitting in their own patch of slime on the back seat. Children love to give you surprises, don't they?

I scoop up everything and hurl it out of sight over my shoulder. Then I resolve to pick up the next hiker I see. Only the next hiker looks very like Hannibal Lector so I resolve not to pick him up and just keep driving. Fast. Hopefully the next one will be young, blonde and look like Reese Witherspoon. Or maybe not. He's an Aussie called Steve and I don't think he's been waiting all morning with a plan to mug me.

'Thanks mate, I'll just shove my bag in the back.'

That'll flatten the apple cores nicely then.

'I'm on a journey to find myself,' he jokes as he jumps in.

'Me too, ' I say as we pull out and drive off.

'Really? Cool. So far I've covered Thailand, Cambodia, the Philippines and China. This is the European bit. Where've you been?'

Either I lie or I tell him.

'Oh, lots of places.'

It wasn't a lie. I have been to lots of places.

'I went to Cambodia once,' I add quickly. Still not lying.

'Really? Great isn't it? I loved those temples up north in the jungle.'

'Up at Angkor?'

'Yea, awesome, man. Had the squits up there most of the time and couldn't get to the dunny but it was a great time. How'd they ever build those things, eh?'

'I met lots of people who lived through Pol Pot.'

'Man, he was a fruitcake, wasn't he? D'you know you got a red light on there, mate? Look, on your dash.'

'I know.'

'Should you be driving with it on?'

'It's fine.'

'It looks like . . . yea, that's the management light.'

'I know.'

'You know what the management is?'

A pause. Should I bluff this one?

'Er, yes.'

'You shouldn't go above forty-four with that light on.'

'I'll bear that in mind.'

'Is that a Bible?'

Oh, things are getting better and better.

I nod but don't say anything. Instead I switch the CD player on cos I know that the music coming out will sound manly.

'My brother's a preacher. Don't go in for it myself but he's all right.'

'Is he a minister?'

'Kind of. He goes about trying to convert people.'

'Does he try and convert you?'

He laughs. 'Sure. All the time. I don't know, why are Christians like that?'

'Like what?'

'You know, always trying to change everybody? I'm happy. I'm cool. Live and let live.'

'But hang on, you said you were trying to find yourself.'

He laughs, but he doesn't say anything in reply, instead he picks up my Bible and thumbs through it.

'I doubt if I'll find myself in here,' he says putting it down again.

'I did.'

'What?'

'I said . . . maybe.'

'If God sorted out the world a bit more I might have a bit more time for him.'

'You reckon?'

'Sure, if he came down and tidied a few things up then yea – I'd listen to him. If he's God, then it wouldn't be difficult to get down here and settle things, get rid of the lowlife and sort out some problems. I guess that means you're one of them then, eh?'

'Which? Lowlife or Christian?'

I joke to avoid the answer but he already knows it.

'Why?' he asks.

'Why? Why am I a Christian?' Now I'm in trouble, I've been asked the dream question and suddenly my carefully thought out theology is seeping out my left ear. Why do I believe? How can I tell it so that he'll believe? I have to convert him. I have to convert him. I have to convert him. I have to build on the years of work his brother must have done. He's probably praying for him right now so make sure you say something that will be clear and relevant and perfectly sum up why Jesus died for the world.

'I can't get away from it.'

Oh, well done. That'll convince him.

'That's it?'

'Well yea, it's just always in my head. It's like God's Someone who's always been hanging around for me. I can't get through the day without looking to him.'

'What's that mean? How can you look at him? Where is he?'

Where is he? Okay think. Think. Where is God? Be profound but keep it simple.

'I dunno. Well, he's everywhere. He's in you.'

He laughs.

'If he is, he's found a good place to hide. I haven't tripped over him.'

'Maybe you're tripping over him now.'

He frowns.

'What? Like where? In you?'

'In me, in this car, in that black book.'

He nods and thinks.

'Can you prove this God thing to me?'

I shake my head.

'No. But that's not the point. No one can prove it, not really. Jesus said if you wanna find it then look hard. But there's no incontrovertible evidence in the world. God's all over the place but only if people open their eyes to spot him.'

He nods, grins and points out the window.

'This'll do me, mate. Thanks for the lift. Nice talking to ya.'

Now that's the conversation I wish I'd had with him. That's the scenario that played in my head. And it had plenty of time to play cos in reality we just sat, listened to my manly music and chatted intermittently about travelling and the places we'd seen and the pregnant girlfriend he'd left back home. And that was it.

That stuff about the management light and Cambodia were just about the only direct quotes. None of the stuff about God.

He was in my car for an hour, I gave him a lift from A to B, but I doubt if I moved him much closer to paradise.

28. Leave Your Brain in a Bucket by the Door

Mark 11:27–33; Mark 12:1–34

It's been a hard day. Jesus is mentally exhausted, he's been playing mind games with the Pharisees and Sadducees all afternoon. Following his recent fracas in the Temple they've been at him like locusts trying to consume him alive.

First it was:

'Who said you could wreck the Temple like that? No true rabbi would do that.'

Jesus looked at their flint-hard faces and considered this. He remembered his cousin, a man who would gladly have wrecked a hundred Temples to get his point across.

'I'll tell you, if you tell me where my cousin John got his authority from.'

Silence. They won't reply. They can't. They daren't say earth but they refuse to say heaven. They give Jesus the evil eye. Peter and James step up beside him for support. He's sandwiched between them, caught between a Rock and a hard man.

So then he told his most violent parable. The killer farmers who take possession of a smallholding and violently abuse anyone who comes to claim it back. The story ends with slaughter and the Pharisees are left chewing their lips and balling their fists. What's he thinking of – how dare he accuse them of killing prophets? So they pumped him about taxes – why should they pay money to a corrupt government?

'What's on the coin?' Jesus demanded.

He held one up so they could all see.

'Is it your head or Caesar's?' The answer had barely slipped from their lips when he snapped back, 'Well, then – give to Caesar what's rightfully his, and keep your questions to yourselves.'

So then they offered him a parable of their own, a convoluted tale about one bride and seven brothers. Who she's gonna end up with in heaven? She married them all on earth but it'll be bigamy up there! Jesus knew it was just a ploy but he still patiently answered them, though his stamina was turning paper thin by then.

And now it's the commandments question. One of the teachers of the law steps up to test him again.

'Master, please tell me which is the most important rule in the law?'

The teacher doesn't look entirely comfortable. Jesus guesses he drew the short straw.

Jesus stares him straight in the face, but as he talks to the guy, his face softens with each word.

'Love your God with all your heart, and with all your soul, and with all your mind and with all your strength. This is the first and the greatest rule. This is the touchstone, the plumbline for good living. And the second one, equally important, is summed up like this.' He glances around at the mixture of fierce and friendly faces. 'Are you listening closely? Okay, here it is. Care for other people. Watch out for them. Serve them. Lift them up. Love them the way you love yourself. Everything that matters is based on these two simple but difficult laws.'

The teacher nods.

'You're right,' he says, 'loving God with all my understanding and every bit of my energy is vital, and living
out that compassion towards other people is crucial.
These two things are much more important than worship offerings.'

Jesus relaxes for the first time that day. The muscles of
his face ease into a crooked grin. It always lifts his spirits when he stumbles across true hunger for the things of
God. As the teacher turns dutifully away, Jesus puts a
hand on his shoulder and pulls him back. He looks him
straight in the face and says, 'My friend, I want to tell
you – you are on the front doorstep of the Kingdom of
God.'

The teacher looks startled and smiles suddenly.
Behind him his work colleagues cuss and start to walk
away. Thankfully, on that bombshell, all bets are off and
all the questions end.

I'm nearly back. And now I start to feel depressed. It's
that end-of-holiday feeling – when you're going away,
the world is full of possibilities: when you're coming
home, it's back to the same old same old. The fields and
houses and superstores start to look dreadfully familiar.
All the mystery's going. I'm not in new places any more,
I'm back in the old. On a whim, I suddenly pull off.
Don't worry, I'm not about to stow aboard a slow plane
to China. I just need to come down slowly. There's an
old café near here that I've driven past countless times
and always wanted to visit. It's in one of those little
towns with a bandstand and a memorial to the
unknown soldier slap in the centre. The café goes by the
name of Blyton's and mercifully it's still open on this
darkening Sunday. I park up and walk in. The bell
jangles, the kind of bell that's been jangling in tea shops

all over England for a very long time. That reassuring sound that makes you feel like a good cup of tea could solve the world's problems. International terrorism, third world debt, underage drinking, no problem. Just warm the pot and crack out the tea cakes. It lulls you into that wonderful sense of false security that you need every so often. This is England and everything's okay. It reminds me of a certain tea shop in *Withnail and I*. Glorious. Half the tables are strewn with Sunday news-papers and monthly magazines. An old man, probably Blyton himself, wanders over as I take a seat and asks me what I'd like. I order the finest tea and a couple of large hot-buttered crumpets. He doesn't write anything down which either means that he is brilliant at his job and doesn't need a pad, or that he's terrible and no one usually comes in here. I thumb through the news and find it's as bad as ever. People's lives seem just as com-plex and catastrophic as they were three days ago. A great man once claimed that it was worth having a paper in one hand and a Bible in the other. One of the things I have come to appreciate about the Bible is its complexity. It contains all the things that we encounter in the paper. Pleasure, pain, triumph, disaster, famine and genocide. Hopefully the reporting is a little more honest, but it doesn't shy away from the tough things. We don't have to put our intellect in the deep freeze when we journey with God. In fact, he wants us to exer-cise those little grey cells. Mind, soul, heart, will and strength. It's a powerful cocktail – but I can't help think-ing that in many Christian circles there's far too much heart in the mix and very little brain.

Jesus had to use his brain on many occasions. Boy, did they put his intellect to the test. On any given day in the Gospels you can find more mental gymnastics than in a month of *Newsnights*. Jesus worked hard and admonished his listeners to do the same. I fear that we miss the point when we just take a few words from the good book and toss them out like a frisbee for others to grab and hurl at someone else. Jesus' words were like his meals and his miracles, signs that pointed to something more. Signs of a kingdom to be explored. Knock, seek and ask. And never stop.

29. The Sound of the Suburbs

2 Corinthians 2:14–17; Hebrews 11:1–40 and Hebrews 12:1

Paul hears a roar from outside and stares out of the window. Another victory procession makes its way down the street. The crowds are out there as ever and here comes the first subdivision. The prisoners. The locals are ready, armed with rotten food and fresh dung, and as the wounded soldiers and unfortunate victims draw alongside them, they let loose with the missiles. Faeces and food splatter across the faces of their enemies. The prisoners duck and dive and do their best to dodge the foul deposits, but they're chained together and no one's going far to avoid the barrage that's coming their way. One or two move so fiercely that they drag some of the others off their feet, for a moment there's a scrum of foreign bodies writhing in the dust and the crowd move in to pelt the sitting targets. The bodies quickly become a mound of greens and browns, as the stinking excrement plasters them from head to foot. Eventually some of the soldiers move in and break up the crowd. A few sharp snags on the chain gets the human zoo back on its feet and they move off again. Humiliation time's over. Their day's almost done. They only have death waiting for them now.

Another roar goes up from the crowd as incense heralds the arrival of the troops. Clouds of purple sweeten
the air and in perfect unison the armoured bodies stamp
their way between the cheering crowds. No one dares
hurl anything now. Instant death would follow any kind
of insult at this stage. More incense and the generals
appear on horseback; severe stallions immaculately
groomed, feathered and cloaked carry the top brass into
town. Trumpets blast and the cheering becomes a chant.
The circus is well and truly in town now.

Paul watches and shudders. How many men have
died in honour of this? How many enemies lost their
heads on the battlefield? How many Romans sacrificed
limbs so everyone here can dance and whoop and
holler?

His mind wanders back to the days when he commended violence. The days he watched proudly as
women and children were abused and shackled and
hurled into prison for the sake of ideology. Men slain
where they stood, their bodies collapsing in pools of
their own bodily fluids. And that one day he'll surely
never forget. The day of the martyr. The day Stephen
gaped up at heaven while Paul's friends ground him
into the earth. Paul had smiled at that murder.
Commended blood spilling in the name of protecting the
old faith. Not any more. Some men choose to fight for
their faith. Paul can't – not now – he can only die for his.

He turns to his old scribe and mutters a few quiet
words. The old man can't hear so he has to repeat them.

'Let's thank God, because we are captives of his fierce
love and like prisoners we are led in a victory parade. But
not in shame, not pelted with corrosive refuse. No, we are
presented with honour and dignity. Like generals and
heroes. Christ is proud to bring us into the city – exam-
ples of his power and goodness. And not only in the city

– wherever we go, he uses us to tell others about the victory he has won and to spread the Good News like expensive perfume. We sweeten the air and brighten the lives of those watching. Our lives are a fragrance presented by Christ to God.

Not everyone appreciates the parade. We remind the friends of God of his goodness and lasting life. But we remind his enemies that death is a reality, that grace is not a cheap perfume, but an expensive gift to be appreciated and relished. Our presence in God's parade is perceived differently by those known to be saved and by those known to be perishing. To those who are perishing we are a fearful stench of death and doom. But to those who are being saved we are a life-giving aroma.

The heroes of our faith have gone before us. Because of their faith some believed and were rescued, others believed and died. All of these people – Abel, Noah, Abraham, Sarah, Isaac, Jacob – received God's approval because of their faith, yet none of them received all that God had promised. For God had far better things in mind for us that would also benefit them, for they can't receive the prize at the end of the race until we finish the race. Therefore, since we are surrounded by such a huge crowd of witnesses, spurring us on, let us strip off every weight that slows us down, especially the sin that so easily hinders our progress. And let us run with endurance the race that God has set before us. Our heroes were far from perfect – yet they ran the race and they call to us. Keep going! Don't give up. If we can do it, so can you.'

I don't expect, of course, to find the flags out and a reformed Jam playing on my roof to welcome me home. My return is certainly no victory parade, although it's some small triumph to see me back so soon. Too soon, it seems, for the house is cold and dark and, though the porch light is on, there's no one home.

Paul would have been very disappointed and would not have been inspired to write to the Corinthians about it all.

So what now? I stand at the door and knock but there's no sign of life. I was kind of hoping for a hug from the kids and an admiring smile from the wife. I've done the right thing. I've come back to be responsible. I'm three days older and maybe four minutes wiser. But I've no audience to prove myself to, no one to impress with this knowledge. I go in, sit in the dark and sip a warm can of coke.

One day I hope to find a welcome in another home. A massive place where they lay on the kind of welcome that's more like an Olympic opening ceremony. One that includes all the technological, wide-screen, pyromaniacal effects in the unknown universe. I fear of course that I might turn up and find I'm not on the guest list. I fear that they'll say there's been some terrible mistake and if I'd just like to get in the lift, it'll take me *down* to the correct floor. It's the kind of fear that can keep a guy awake at four in the morning. Perhaps there'll be a tradesman's entrance. Or maybe I'll be allowed in through a gap in the fence. Or a back door for those of us who dabbled in the faith. All too often these days I realise I haven't lived what I believed. How can I have the kind of faith that buys into honesty, compassion and courage, yet still be so dishonest, selfish and scared? I'm good in the spotlight when I have an audience, but when it actually comes to washing feet, fighting fights and running races, I'm up there in the commentary box, wincing, groaning and giving out advice. I hope I'm in that procession. I so hope so.

Life often turns out differently to the way you expect. It's not black and white. It's grey, and not just one shade of grey, but a hundred, a thousand, a million. And it's not fair either. And when I feel like this there's only one place left to go.

Cutter's.

The old pirate will comfort me; the fire and the chair and the old gnarled landlord, they'll make me feel better. I grab my coat and take a hike down the road. Two and a half days ago I drove down it and headed for freedom. Now I'm back, has anything changed? Am I different? Am I a better person? The truth is, I'm still me. I drove away with me and I've come back with me.

But we all do that. We like to think we can become Superman or Spiderman, or Bond or Batman – but they're not true heroes, they're not biblical heroes. Biblical heroes are like me – broken, frustrated, successful and sad. Frightened but trusting, strong but weak. The world has only ever produced one Man who was any different and even he chose to walk the way of the normal guy. We're all God has ever had, dusty, egotistical, inspired, fat-headed, kind-hearted men. And apparently, in spite of everything and against all odds, he believes we can change the world.

So I buy a pint of Guinness, nod at the old crumpled landlord and settle by the fire in my favourite chair in Cutter's. I sigh and watch the flames for a while. That's better. Now I am home. I pull out my old battered book and begin again.

If you look hard enough, the little black leatherback won't let you down. Horror, drama, action, adventure, romance, sex, comedy, mystery, war. You can find the whole shooting match. It's all in there. There's even a science fiction section at the end.

I flip to the opening credit sequence in Judges and find a suitably action-packed beginning.

The men of Judah have surrounded the town of Bezek and are preparing to assault the town. They battle long and hard and eventually break through the defences to take the town.

The king, Adoni-bezek escapes, but the Israelites give chase and track him down. They soon capture him, pin him to the ground and cut off his thumbs and big toes. To which Adoni-bezek replies, 'I once had seventy kings with thumbs and big toes cut off, eating scraps from under my table. Now God has paid me back for what I did to them.'

Although what he actually said was, 'Aggggh! I once had ow! Seventy youch! Kings with thumbs and aggghh! Big tooooooooes! cut off aggggggghhhhhh . . .'